M000208137

Enjoy!

A Life By the Sea

A Life By the Sea

Modern American Seafood by Chef Dean James Max

Photography by Quentin Bacon

Book Design by Joshua C. Chen

DJM Publishing

Boca Raton, Florida

Copyright © 2005 by Dean James Max

Photography copyright © 2005 by Quentin Bacon Photography

Design copyright © 2005 by Chen Design Associates

All rights reserved. No part of this book may be reproduced
in any form without written permission from the publisher.

ISBN 0-9764369-0-6

Printed in China

Designed by Chen Design Associates, San Francisco
www.chendesign.com

DJM Publishing
1167 SW 3rd Street
Boca Raton, FL 33486
561.367.7654
deanjamesmax@yahoo.com
www.deanjamesmax.com

First Printing 2005
Second Printing 2006

Manufactured by
Favorite Recipes® Press
An imprint of

FRP

P.O. Box 305142
Nashville, Tennessee 37230
1.800.358.0560

To my wife, Amy, and children Remy and Jace

who support me in this ever demanding career

To my mother, Joni

who always made the kitchen a loving place to be

To be in the tropics is pure pleasure for me!

The autumn leaves and snow are great during vacation,

but I prefer the healthy feeling of the warm sun,

gentle breezes, and salty waters of a Southern coastal town.

The Sea has always been a refuge for me.

A place to calm my nerve

The tranquility

can wash away all the stress in my world.

and escape into a world of dreams.
f a blue sky and crystal blue waters

There is something about the water
which is magical to me
I feel it, like a magnet, pulling me to its edge
and when I am within it...
I am never without a smile.

My love of food is fed from the fond memories of smells and tastes of my childhood. When I smell the stem of a vine ripe tomato, I can visualize myself running through the large rows of tomato plants as my brother and I played hide and seek. The taste of a cucumber brings to mind my father who used to carry a salt shaker and pocketknife through the fields to enjoy the simplicity of such a subtle vegetable. The smell of a leek reminds me of sitting with my mother and helping sort the seedlings to be replanted.

So many smells and tastes zoom my mind to childhood memories. The excitement of having an omelet from a double yolk chicken egg... the simple taste of a sunfish from the pond... the neighbor get-togethers to feast on local clams and blue crabs... the fresh pomegranate my brother and I grabbed from Mr. Beasley's tree on the way back from fishing...

Above right:
Driving a tractor
at age 10 with my
brother Charlie.

I have to attribute my fearlessness toward hard work to the not-so-fond memories of being on a farm. You have never prayed so hard for rain until you have to move sections of irrigation pipe over sixty acres of peppers every four hours at the age of ten. I would have to miss cartoons on Saturday mornings so I could cultivate the field with the tractor before the sun became too strong. Through the hard work of growing up on a farm, I have found serenity and comfort in the preparation of food. When I am stressed, I would much rather turn a case of artichokes or filet sixty pounds of fish. That is my thinking zone—that is my spa.

Left: Harvesting
lettuce at age 6
with my sister Tami.

I grew up on a small farm in the rural town of Machipango, on Virginia's eastern shore. The small town was nestled between the Chesapeake Bay and the Atlantic. This area is known for its oysters, clams, striped bass, flounder, and most notorious blue crab. I can remember racing my brother to check the crab pots for the possibility of snagging a soft-shell. The winner

Above: My Dad, Charles Jr., a true farmer at heart, in our cabbage patch.

Right: My Mother, Joni, telling stories at her dinner party.

would gloat while eating the special treat sautéed on country bread with mayonnaise and vine ripe tomatoes. It still amuses me to see people at the restaurant try to pick the meat out of a sautéed soft-shell. I guess I just take some things for granted.

The shore was the beginning of my gravitation towards the sea and my love for seafood. I grew up with the simple flavors of drum fish and corn, blue crab and old bay, oysters and horseradish, soft-shells and brown butter, and Flounder with crabmeat. My vacations were spent with my grandparents at their bed and breakfast on the Jersey Shore near Cape May. My grandfather, who had been a chef in New York, was always cooking something grand. There were always fresh soup stocks brewing in their kitchen, and special sauces he was straining. His favorite pastime was teaching us how to fish. I can still remember loading the boat with funny-looking flounder.

In my teens, we moved to the small coastal town of Stuart in southern Florida. My dad had decided that brokering produce was a little more stable and a lot more lucrative. So he started his own company selling Florida produce to grocery store chains all over the country. This was my first lesson in the value of fresh produce. His customers would actually pay more to get the produce that was the newest from the field and the best quality. Of course, my brother and I were the chosen ones to travel all across the state and inspect the products we were selling. I would actually sit there at the packing house and make sure that a particular lot of corn that I saw just come from the field was loaded on to our trucks. There is an amazing difference between the flavor of the same seed of corn grown on two different farms, as there is a difference between the aroma of produce just picked from the field versus food that has been sitting for five days in the packing house cooler. Anyone who has eaten corn from a roadside stand can attest to the pleasure of that.

My excitement for cooking has to come from my mom. She is a great cook and I always enjoyed helping her in the kitchen. We were always doing something exciting with food.

Whether it was making eggs in a basket, or brining pickling cucumbers in a large trash can, I was always learning. Even in high school, when I worked as a bus boy in our local French restaurant, I wanted to be in the kitchen. My dad being a businessperson at heart insisted I get a business degree from college. After four-and-a-half years at Florida State University, I went my way with a marketing degree in hand. My passion for cooking would only increase after a visit to Florence, Italy. I was fortunate to take courses at the highly-acclaimed Hospitality School and spent the rest of my time studying art, food, and having fun of course. I really feel that my experience in Italy brought out my creative side, which had been waiting in the wings. My travels through Spain, France, Germany, Greece and most of the great cities of Europe had helped me to understand the importance of impeccable product, and the simplicity of traditional combinations. After returning from Europe with the thoughts of risotto, marinated octopus, rouget with basil aioli, and many other flavors I just couldn't forget, I had come to that fork in the road that any true epicurean faces at some point in their life. I could work for my dad and come home from my nine-to-five job and spend hours of enjoyment cooking in my kitchen at home, or I could leave the money, weekends, nights off, and regular life style behind to live within my passion. For me it was an easy choice. I had to at least walk down this road, even if I had to run back screaming later in life.

After visiting the Culinary Institute of America in Hyde Park, New York, I really felt I needed to start working with talented chefs. I started at a French haute cuisine restaurant in Atlanta called 103 West, and quickly moved to the Ritz-Carlton Hotel Company where I moved about the country working under very talented chefs including Daniel Shaffhauser and two-Michelin-star Gerard Pangaud. After moving with the Ritz to gain more knowledge, I took my first chef position at the Brasserie Savoy in the Savoy Hotel, San Francisco. The ethnic diversity of San Francisco offered me as a growing chef innumerable new ideas. Just to be in an area where I was exposed to the differences of so many creative chefs gave me more direction within myself.

The Brasserie Savoy was a modern French brasserie. I used a French approach to such great western treasures like Columbia River sturgeon, Washington king salmon, Oregon snails, diver scallops, abalone, and spot prawns. Great oysters and Dungeness crab were a staple. The Pacific Ocean provided an open playground with new seafood, and the organic farmers markets offered the freshest of the land to pair with the sea. These were the golden years of learning for me. I returned to Atlanta to open Mumbo Jumbo with acclaimed chef Gunter Seeger as my partner. There we created a menu that had no cultural boundaries. Like its name, Mumbo Jumbo the restaurant was a mixing of different cultural flavors. After a very successful opening during the 1996 Summer Olympic Games, I could start to feel my longing for the sea. I missed the markets of the west and the fever I felt from the idea of creating. I left Atlanta to move to Brentwood in Los Angeles, where I became the Executive Chef of Woodside restaurant. At Woodside, I was able to nurture a relationship with a 20-acre garden at the Veterans Hospital across the street. There, the horticulturist, Ida, and I, with the help of many veterans, turned the direction of the garden. We started to produce baby lettuces, Swiss chard, lemongrass, shiso, and the newest craze, micro-greens. Woodside was the restaurant where I felt the closest to my guests. A small neighborhood restaurant with an open kitchen gave me the ability to reach out to my customers and feel their response to the food. After three years in that great location my wife and I, now with a new child and one more on the way, had an opportunity in Florida we could not resist. We could now be near our families, and I was given an open slate to create a seafood restaurant in Marriott's Harbor Beach Resort and Spa. The concept was to open 3030 Ocean, a modern seafood restaurant where we would source the highest quality purveyors and create an ever-changing menu representing the best of what each moment has to offer. We would operate like a street restaurant both in production and marketing. To have the support of a large company and the flexibility of a small restaurant would be the best of both worlds for a chef.

Right:
My Grandfather
Stephen Lesko, who
was a chef and avid
fisherman.

Below:
My Grandfather
Charles Max, who
was a farmer in
northern New Jersey.
This was a photo for
a Lucky Strikes ad.

Some people ask me, "Why change?" It is a simple answer. I change to experience the dawn of new discoveries. I always run into that old school waiter who is opposed to anything beyond a classic. Why serve anything but potatoes gratin and mint jelly with your lamb? When it works, it works. Do not fuss with it. Beef with béarnaise, sole with lemon butter, trout with almonds, and the list goes on. I am sure he is the same type that goes to that same cabin in the mountains he has been visiting for the last twenty years. What if Columbus thought the Portugal coast was the most beautiful thing to see in the summer, and there was no reason to go anywhere else. What if Caesar Cardini thought that lettuce only needs red wine vinegar and olive oil? Why ruin perfectly good Romaine leaves? All of the classics in their day were new adventures. It is our job as modern chefs to find the new classics. In saying "What if?" we are all looking for that new lobster Thermidor or oysters Rockefeller. That is what we live for, and that is the center of our excitement.

Modern American Seafood is three words:

MODERN! Born of our concerns today, the idea of a healthy life, the balance of what foods we eat, and how it affects our active lifestyles. Our desire to see beauty in ourselves, our lives, and our food. Our need for stimulation and variety. A mix of our past, our present, and a representation of current times.

AMERICAN! The pride of a nation where all is welcome, a culture of diversity, a melting pot, a fusion of ideas. A place where everything goes and the limits are always tested. An interest in others and what they are doing. Endless curiosity. Sophisticated but not

Clockwise from top left:
Edible banana flowers.
At a typical local
seafood hangout.
Tropical palm leaves.
A quirky cafe in
farm country.
A house of fish scales.
Having a laugh.

stuffy. Relaxed yet determined. Traditional but still bold, demanding but always appreciative. America is conservative openness. We need to know it all, experience it all, and solve it all. America is the Reese's® cups candy. The chocolate that fell in the peanut butter and made all our lives better.

SEAFOOD! The soul of another world, the treasure from that magnetic vastness which pulls me closer to its edge, the life from a sea of childhood memories, the mystery of creatures so complicated and beautiful, the bounty from a world of serenity, darkness, and enlightenment.

These three words come together to explain the unlimited possibilities of seafood cuisine. The ideas of modern lightness, intensities of flavor, simplicity, and freshness all meet with the combination of American diversity and openness, and plunge deep to the bottom of the darkest oceans where all is to be adored.

The Mind of A Modern Chef

We are always looking at new possibilities, that new great idea, that "wow" that makes people stop and smile. I feel that these discoveries are like treasures, and the only way to find them is to keep digging. You cannot force it. My creative development always begins with the ingredient. People always ask me, "What is your specialty?" My specialty is the passion I have for the flavor of food. It does not stop at one culture, and it cannot be fenced by only a group of regional items.

When I see fresh blue crab and smell its aroma, my mind wanders to the taste of the sweet crunchiness of the crab with the salty depth of smoked bacon, and the watery freshness of a summer tomato. The soft aioli smeared bread is a sponge where all the flavors meet to enchant. I can see myself on an old wooden dock looking out over calm water filled with sailboats, long narrow skiffs, and a maze of crab pot buoys. As I think of my dish, the tomato stands out and I begin to reminisce over a bready tomato gazpacho I had in Barcelona. I think of the creaminess of this non-dairy marriage and I can imagine how tasty the crab and bacon would be with that. In my approach, I think elegant and beautiful. A fantastic chilled bowl with a pool of thick gazpacho made from the freshest heirloom tomatoes, sweet and spicy peppers, summer cucumbers, yeasty bread and Mediterranean herbs. In the center of the soup, a napoleon of Maryland crabmeat, smokey bacon, and micro-greens finished with a drizzle of fresh pressed virgin olive oil, cracked salt, and freshly ground pepper.

Buoys and lobster crates
waiting for season to open.

Clockwise from top left:
Harvesting striped bass at
the Everglades Fish Farm.
Peter Jarvis of Triar Seafood
showing his best catch.
Fish cutter at Triar with
a 100-pound ahi tuna.
A Key West lobsterman
showing me how his traps
work. Sorting the bass into
an ice bath. Howard Rau,
showing off his latest golden
crab catch.

In my mental journey, I can visualize my painting, and in every artist's work lies a piece of his thoughts and experiences. Some customers ask me, "What makes the business of cooking so stressful?" The stress of our art is so difficult due to its changing nature. We are measured by consistency. An oil painter creates his masterpiece in an easily controlled environment, and hangs his soul on a wall to be viewed. A sculptor does the same, with only the concern of what vantage the viewer should take. An architect designs, redesigns, builds, and lets his art reflect his view of the world for all to see and measure in the change of time. Whereas, I have my vision of gazpacho with Maryland Crab Napoleon, and in my art a dish can change from night to night, from hour to hour, from table to table, all on the whim of a focused or unfocused cook. The chef is there to design, redesign, sample, measure consistency, and at the end of the night his art is only a memory in the stomachs of those he fed. I hope they were good thoughts!

Respect your Food!

Growing up on a farm instilled in me a certain respect for food. I know the hard work that goes into growing what we eat. In our modern society, we see everything pre-packaged, pre-cooked, and portion-sized. Some people even forget the fact that it is a chicken that gave its breast for that plastic-coated package. Let us face it, we are all a part of the food chain. The kindest thing you can do is respect the fact that the chicken gave its life for your enjoyment and nourishment. I teach all my cooks how to handle the food in a manner that is understanding of its sacrifice. We treat each item with care to present it to the customer in its most natural state. Great meats and seafood do not need to be marinated. Have you ever noticed that some of your most flavorful food memories are those you created with the ultimate product you were provided? It could have been the grilled fish you caught that afternoon, the peaches you picked and made into ice cream, or the garden herbs that flavored your pasta which were your connection with eating something directly from its source. We are always reminding ourselves of that connection. That is why we choose suppliers who share our philosophy concerning the product we handle. When you work with food every day, it becomes easy to lose that focus on product. We choose small companies that specialize in doing a few things well. There is one person who gets our oysters and a woman in Maine who has great mussels. We have one company for our goat cheese and a different one for our blue cheese. The specialty of our product is what truly makes the difference. The simplicity of our food would not work without it. Sourcing for us is a constant search to learn more about a particular product and who can get it to us in the fastest way. How can someone who carries meat, eggs, salmon, and cardboard boxes be providing me with items of ultimate integrity? We rely on our suppliers to educate us further on each product, every step of the way. When I talk to my tomato person in San Diego, he assures me that I will not be happy with the heirloom tomatoes this week. They need one more week to be at their peak. I have to be able to trust him and I will wait. When my fish person calls to tell me they are catching the first school of the mighty Block Island swordfish off the coast of Boston, my mind begins to wander with possibilities. This northern swordfish will feed off the rich shelf of the George's Bank before its migration to spawn. It is fattening up like a bear since it will not eat much on its travel to their spawning site. Some lucky customers will get to enjoy the sublime taste of the fattiest, most flavorful swordfish the world has to offer.

That is why we keep it simple. When you understand better what you are getting, don't you want to savor it? Sometimes we lose our savoring ability because we neglect to create a longing for foods. We are used to getting food from all over the world. It sounds great, a season that never ends. I have Australian Barramundi fish come out of the water, into ice, and sitting on my doorstep 35 hours later. You would have to be in Queensland to get better than that. The problem with that is two-fold. Do you really think they are going to airfreight items like green beans from Guatemala, or asparagus from Chile, in a way where you will see the product faster than two weeks from harvest? We also lose the fun of the seasons. We are like Veruca Salt in Willy Wonka's chocolate factory, "I want it all and I want it now!" The pleasure of a Georgia peach is that no amount of money in the world will bring that peach to market any sooner. We actually need our government to step in and create seasons for us. When stone crab season starts, we are all waiting for the first bite of that sweet salty treat. We need to give species a time to breathe and reproduce. The United States does a great job on controlling our fishing. I am sure to some anglers, too good of a job. Reports on eastern swordfish have been better; however, when in open waters off the Chilean coast we cannot control the poaching of over fifty percent of the Chilean sea bass catch, many chefs across the land choose to pull this incredibly popular fish off their menu. I do not want to be a part of killing off an entire species. Everything should have a season, except maybe salt and pepper.

Brand Names

Why do chefs use so many brand names on their menus? Niman Ranch Lamb, Block Island Swordfish, George's Bank Scallops, Coach Farm Goat Cheese, Gulf of Mexico Tuna, White Water Clams, Turks and Caicos Queen Conch, Bouchot Mussels, and the list never stops. It is telling you our concern to get you the best of the best. We are either featuring a product or purveyor that tells you to expect the best. It is like buying Versace or Valentino. You expect a higher level of artisanship both from grower and nature. Even in such mainstream areas as salmon farming, there are

Clockwise from left: Inspecting a tomato patch in Homestead, Florida. Young native coconuts. The beauty of tropical bamboo.

differences between the competition. The quality of the feed they get will reflect their flavor, and we will pay a premium to get the best. This is what gives us the ability to savor. I can remember eating chicken in France for the first time. How could that be so good? It did not seem real. We search for someone like Bell and Evans who raises chickens in a more natural way. I can remember when I was a cook at the Ritz-Carlton and got the promotion to work in the kitchen of Gerard Pangaud. I was expecting this two-Michelin-starred chef to be creating the craziest combinations known to man. I was shocked to see the simplicity and I soon came to understand the importance of ingredients. Our scallops came live in their shells and would quiver when I sliced them. Relax, I have a heart. I face each lobster before their death and hope they feel no pain, and I know they will leave this world making someone very happy. Who knows? I could come back in their shell one day, and I can guarantee that the court bouillon looks better from outside the pot. I will eat him anyway, and when I cook, store, and prepare him, I will keep in mind that he could have lived fifty years to get here today.

Modern Simplicity

Modern simplicity describes the ability to pair textures and flavors in such a subtle way as to not confuse the direction of the dish. Simplicity can be the result of a complicated path. In search for a sauce to complete a dish of red snapper, grilled green onions, and Caribbean boniato, I consider the simple refreshing flavor of carrot sauce. I think about the style of sauce with the dish. Snapper is a lean fish with a light flavor, and I want to keep the overall light feel. It still needs some zest to the dish. Thinking of the regional parts of this dish, Central American boniato, green onions, and snapper, I choose to add orange juice, garlic, and cumin to my sauce to give it a sweet spicy appeal.

Combinations

To figure out what combinations work well together, I suggest looking at cultural foods. These are known combinations that mix well with each other. Ingredients that have been put together by nature and have been paired with one another for centuries. It is like learning to play music. You first learn your scales, or the notes that sound good together, and then you can work outside that when you have the basics down. The same goes with food. If you know that combining red pepper, fennel, eggplant, zucchini, thyme, tomato, garlic, and rosemary are a Mediterranean or warm climate combination, you can experiment safely in that musical harmony without going out of tune.

Left: Beautiful star fruit.
Right: Dayboat Virginia wild striped bass.

COMBINATIONS OF THE WORLD

ITALY

almonds	mushrooms
artichokes	nectarines
asparagus	olive oil
black pepper	onions
broccoli raab	parsley
cabbage	pasta
capers	pine nuts
cardoons	pumpkin
celery	radicchio
cherries	red peppers
chestnuts	risotto
chick peas	rosemary
corn	sage
dry cheese	spinach
dry chili	squash blossoms
eggplant	swiss chard
eggs	tomatoes
fennel	walnuts
garlic	whey cheese
green beans	white beans
leeks	white truffles
lemon	zucchini
melons	

Seafood

anchovies	sardines
calamari	sea urchin
cuttlefish	shrimp
monkfish	snails
mussels	swordfish
red mullet	trout
salt cod	tuna

JAPAN

asparagus	miso
avocado	onions
bamboo shoots	plums
beet	rice
bok choy	sake
broccoli	sea weed
carrot	sesame
celery	shiso
chilis	soba
chives	soy sauce
cilantro	sprouts
cucumber	tofu
daikon	tomato
dashi	wasabi
eggplant	watercress
garlic	Yuzu juice
green onion	

abalone	oysters
clams	salmon
crabs	sardines
eels	scallops
fish eggs	sea bass
flounder	sea urchin
hamachi	shrimp
lobster	snapper
mackerel	squid
monkfish	tuna
octopus	

FRANCE

artichokes	mushrooms
asparagus	olives
baby onions	parsley
beets	pears
berries	peppers
cabbage	plums
carrots	potatoes
cauliflower	pumpkin
celery	radishes
cheese	rhubarb
cherries	rosemary
corn	salsify
cucumbers	shallots
eggplant	sorrel
eggs	spinach
endive	tarragon
fava beans	thyme
fennel	tomatoes
garlic	truffles
green beans	turnips
leeks	watercress
lemon	white beans
lentils	zucchini
lettuce	

anchovies	sardines
blue lobster	scallops
caviar	sea urchin
crayfish	shrimp
frogs legs	smoked salmon
loup de mer	snails
monkfish	squid
mussels	trout
oysters	turbot
rouget	

Use this table as a guide to learn the foods that will blend well with each other. It's only a guideline — not the law. Each ingredient — like notes in a musical scale — flow together and create magic!

THAILAND & INDONESIA

banana	limes
banana blossom	mango
basil	mint
bean sprouts	mung bean
bok choy	mushrooms
broccoli	mustard
cauliflower	Napa cabbage
celery	noodles
chili	palm sugar
chives	papaya
cilantro	peanuts
coconut milk	pineapple
cucumber	red & green
daikon	curry paste
eggplant	rice
eggs	rice noodles
galangal	scallions
garlic	sesame
ginger	shallots
hot peppers	spinach
kaffir lime leaf	tamarind
lemongrass	tomatoes

CHINA

almonds	mung beans
basil	mushrooms
bok choy	noodles
broccoli	onions
cabbage	orange
chili	parsley
cilantro	pears
daikon	rice
eggplant	seaweed
fermented beans	sesame
garlic	Sichuan pepper
ginger	snow peas
hoisin	spinach
kumquat	tomatoes
lemon	turnips
lemongrass	water chestnuts
lychee	watercress
mango	zucchini

LATIN AMERICA

avocado	mint
banana leaves	mushrooms
bananas	olives
basil	onions
carrots	orange
chili	oregano
chocolate	papaya
cilantro	parsley
cinnamon	passion fruit
coconut	plantains
coffee	pumpkin
corn	radishes
culantro	raisins
cumin	rum
eggplant	shallots
garlic	strawberry
ginger	sugar cane
guava	tamarind
honey	tomatillo
jalapeno	tomato
lime	vanilla
mango	yams
melons	

Seafood

THAILAND & INDONESIA

catfish	mussels
clams	octopus
crabs	red fish
dried fish	rock cod
eel	shrimp
fish sauce	shrimp paste
lobster	snapper
mackerel	squid

CHINA

catfish	rock cod
clams	salmon
crab	scallops
lobster	shrimp
mussels	squid
oysters	tuna

LATIN AMERICA

crab	snapper
lobster	squid
mussels	tuna
octopus	
sea bass	
shrimp	

Balance

Left: Inspecting papaya
at a local market.
Right: A catch of the
Florida golden crab.

Now that we have the broad idea of what combinations of ingredients work well together, we can match them to make a well-balanced dish. Balance in your food is what makes it exciting and enjoyable. I want you to take away more from this book than some seafood recipes which you will never remember to carry with you to the store. Instead, take the idea of what makes these recipes work and come up with your own creations.

The idea of balance is nothing new. It lies everywhere in our lives. A Sunday afternoon nap is replenishing because of the stressful work week or the screaming kids around the house. That same idea can be applied to a smooth and silky avocado. Its taste has more flavor with a squeeze of acidic lime and salt. If you napped all day, everyday, it would not deliver the same pleasure. When you taste food, your tongue is processing sweet, salty, spicy, and sour. Your mouth also feels for texture, like crunchy, smooth, juicy, crispy, warm, hot, cold, and freezing. As a chef, I am always looking for the balance in a sauce, garnish, as well as a preparation. When you think of seafood preparation, you only have to know a few essential things to make your own culinary judgments. Think about the fat content and the life habits of the creature. It is no wonder the Chilean sea bass (Patagonian toothfish) is a super fatty fish. It lives in icy cold waters off the Southern Hemisphere. Even if it was a fast swimming fish it could not burn off the fat used to keep it comfortable in those chilly waters. When you are looking for the combination to match an oily fish like sea bass, you must consider the balance. The fish will bring the smooth fattiness to the plate. It will need something acidic, sweet, or spicy to contrast its texture. Even the preparation is important. High heat roasting to render its fat or grilling will help to dry the fish out. It also tastes better with a crispy grilled or sautéed surface, which contrasts the soft buttery texture of its flesh.

The reason we will ship in live Maine lobsters instead of using the Florida spiny lobster outside our door is for their level of sweetness. The fat in the cold water lobster give it more flavor and keeps it more tender. The warm water of the south and its migration habits leave the spiny lobster lean and tough when cooked, and prowling fish like the mahi mahi or wahoo tend to be lean as well. We make sure to undercook them slightly and serve them with something creamy or buttery. Creamy, to me, is a texture, which you can get from all kinds of methods. It can be the sweet creaminess of carrots puréed with olive oil. I prefer to use vegetables as filler for cream and butter. In some dishes, I demonstrate the versatility of texture

Clockwise from top left:
Finger bananas.
Florida's fruit of the
sea — the red snapper.
Baby leeks at harvest.
The beauty of tropical
custard fruit.
Seasonal papayas.
Exotic citrus.

within one ingredient. I can serve soft confit of fennel bulb with a crunchy raw salad of shaved fennel and peppers, a smooth purée of fennel, garlic, thyme, and olive oil, fried fennel fronds, and a drizzle of reduced fennel juice and Pernod. One of my favorites of Gerard Pangaud's desserts was the demonstration of the total usage of an Indian river grapefruit. We served a pinwheel of grapefruit segments drizzled with a reduction of grapefruit juice and Sauterne, centered with a tower of grapefruit aspic, grapefruit sorbet, and topped with thin batons of candied grapefruit zest. In this dish, if you do not have a great grapefruit, what do you have?

Whatever you do, do not go to the store expecting to make something specific. That is where you find that your market does not have the vegetable you need, or the fish did not look that good or they were out of that herb. Look at the seafood available, choose what you love that looks bright and firm that particular day. When you have chosen something that is obviously fresh, shop to find what will match with it. Some things should be bought by price. When artichokes are cheap, you know they are in season. That is when you buy them.

Let's say we found some Alaskan halibut with its white firm textured flesh, which is not oily and will need something buttery to pair with its dryer tendencies. You want to cook it with moistness in mind. Poaching, steaming, and braising are a better idea for this lean fish. You could still grill the halibut, but do not overcook it rendering all of its moisture, and try to pair it with something fatty like a butter sauce or aioli.

You would also choose vegetables that had some crunchiness to add to the soft texture of the fish. When thinking of the vegetables, also consider the balance. Choose within the seasons and think of a regional theme. We get great halibut in the late summer and I like to pair it with the earthiness of artichokes, pearl onions, mushrooms, and spinach. I then pair it with something acidic like a light pinot noir sauce. Any combination will work if you use fresh ingredients and balance them well.

There is also the consideration of temperature that intrigues the senses. When your tongue experiences the change in temperature from something warm to something cold, to something hot, to something freezing, it keeps the sensitivity alive. Sounds like a lot to think about when cooking. It actually does not take much time when you get used to it.

What is happening in the chef's mind?

The whole idea is to be able to walk through the store and come up with your dish at that moment. Start with a basic search. I want some type of seafood salad. You get to the store and see nice large shrimp on sale. Now, we know it's going to be a shrimp salad. It is safer to choose the type of dressing when we know what will be in the salad. I love asparagus and they are so elegant, but they are coming from Chile and at $4.50 a bunch. I think I will keep looking. Wow, the fennel looks great, and it is cheap, and the red peppers are local and perfect. I need some onion flavor to mellow out the sweet vegetables. There is some great sweet Vidalia onions, but will that be too much sweet? We can always balance that later. If they are in season and nice, let's get them.

What about this beautiful white corn? Farm fresh cucumbers, they will work perfect. How about something starchy? I am not sure if I want potato, pasta, or maybe even couscous. Let us wait to figure out the dressing. So far, we have sweet on the corn, peppers, fennel, and onion. We have a watery crunchy neutral with the cucumber. It will add more texture than strong flavor. We need some salty, spicy, and sour. For salty, I could use a nut, which would give me some crunchy as well: pecans, walnuts, cashews, pine nuts, and peanuts? I think I will go with peanuts since I like their flavor with corn. I cannot think of anything sour to go in there, so we can go that direction in the dressing. How about a red wine vinaigrette. What about that red curry I have in my cupboard at home to add some spiciness? I think I will add it to my vinaigrette, but the directions said to cook it. I could still sauté it with some peanut oil and garlic to enhance that flavor and then finish my vinaigrette.

The salad is starting to feel a bit Asian-inspired. So maybe I should use rice wine vinegar or lime juice instead of the red wine vinegar. What kind of herb should I use? I love dill and corn, but I think cilantro or basil would be better for the Asian theme. Since I am going Asian, I think I will use a rice noodle. Maybe I could go back to the produce section and use some of that leafy bok choy. Should I put back the fennel? That seems more Mediterranean. You could, but you do not have to, you never know what you might discover. Now we have come up with:

Fresh shrimp salad with rice noodles, white corn, cucumbers, red pepper, sweet onions, roasted peanuts, bok choy, and red curry vinaigrette

Not bad for 5 minutes in the store!

Enjoying a farm fresh papaya smoothie at Homestead farm stand.

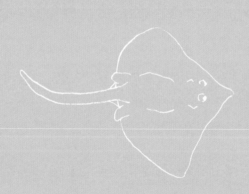

SOFT :: DELICATE :: SWEET :: LEAN

halibut › pg. 56

SEAFOOD GLOSSARY

SKATE

I really like to eat skate. Most people are very confused about this fish. Its texture is very soft and delicate. It has a truly sweet scallop flavor, due to its diet of mollusks on the ocean floor. Even though poaching is a popular preparation for this fish, I like to give it more texture with a spicy cracked coriander crust and a nutty flavor from the browning butter. The chewy nature of lentils add a balance to the skate's soft flesh, and the creamy onion flavor of the leek are a good balance with its sweetness. The jolt of acidity from the red wine vinaigrette balance the buttery feel of the dish.

HALIBUT

I am not a big fan of masking the flavors of fish with thick crusts and coatings, but they can really help the fish to stay moist. I usually prefer the flavor of halibut raw because of its tendency to become dry and flavorless when cooked through. This mushroom crust will help to baste the fish as the butter melts off during the cooking process. The combination of the zucchini, mushroom, and chicken based sauce give the whole dish a uniform earthiness.

TURBOT

Turbot is probably the most prized of the flat fish family due to its moist firm flesh and great flavor. The mineral taste of the spinach and acidity of the vinaigrette bring out the flavor of the fish. The earthiness and spiciness of the cauliflower break up the mildness of the other flavors with out overpowering them.

DOVER SOLE

This would have to be the turbot's stiff competition for the best of the flat fish. Sole is delicate and tasty but can be easily dried-out or overpowered. The earthiness of the garnish share the spotlight and the buttery sauce will help to keep the fish moist. The truffles add elegance to this dish, but do not overshadow the simple joy of the sole. The light bitterness of the white asparagus and field-fresh flavor of the cabbage and peas give the dish plenty of variety. Buy the Dover sole whole from your fishmonger so you can tell for sure it is fresh and not frozen. Look at the eyes for clarity, and look at the gills for red freshness. Frozen fish will have cloudy, dirty eyes, and the gills will be brown. Remember a slimy fish can mean it is super fresh not spoiled.

WILD TURBOT
with curried cauliflower, apples, and lemon vinaigrette

6 wild turbot fillets (*7 oz. each*)

1 lb Savoy style baby spinach

4 Tbs olive oil

2 heads cauliflower

1 green apple (*peeled and sliced*)

½ Tbs Madras curry

2 shallots (*minced*)

1 cup chicken stock (*see pg. 168*)

8 Tbs butter

1 Tbs white truffle oil
(*source: specialty grocer*)

2 oz heavy cream

1 lemon

1 cup lemon vinaigrette (*see pg. 177*)

Break apart the cauliflower and pick out 30 perfect florets for the plates. Put the rest of the cauliflower in salted boiling water and cook it until tender. Drain and transfer the cauliflower to a blender with 2 tablespoons of butter, the heavy cream, and white truffle oil. Purée the mixture until smooth. Season the purée with salt and lemon juice. Keep the purée warm until needed. Blanch the perfect cauliflower pieces in fresh salted boiling water for 2 minutes. Cool them in ice water. Mince the shallots and sweat them in a large non-stick sauté pan with 3 tablespoons of butter over a medium heat. Peel and slice the apple and add it to the shallots. Sprinkle the mixture with the curry and sauté for 20 more seconds. Add the cauliflower and chicken stock and cook until the stock has evaporated. Season with salt and pepper.

Heat a cast iron or steel sauté pan over medium high heat. Season the turbot with salt and pepper. Place a couple of tablespoons of olive oil in the pan and carefully add the fish. Cook the fish for 3 minutes and then flip them. Add 2 tablespoons of butter to the pan and with a spoon, baste the fish with the melting butter. The fish will need only another minute or two to cook. Transfer the fish to a warm plate until ready to serve. In a clean non-stick pan, melt 2 tablespoons of olive oil with 2 tablespoons of butter over a medium high heat. When the butter begins to foam, add the spinach. Season the spinach with salt and pepper. Only wilt the spinach for 30 seconds.

To serve, place some of the spinach on the center of six plates. Put a couple of spoonfuls of the cauliflower purée next to the spinach. Place some of the curried cauliflower and apple on top of the purée. Lay a piece of fish on top of each pile of spinach. Spoon some of the lemon vinaigrette around each fish.

PREP **30 MINUTES**
COOK **15 MINUTES**
SERVES **6**

SPOTTED SKATE WING

with creamy leeks, beluga lentils, and red wine vinaigrette

6 skate fillets *(7 oz each)*
2 Tbs grapeseed oil
8 Tbs butter
3 Tbs cracked coriander seeds
6 oz beluga lentils
3 cups water
1 small carrot *(diced)*
1 small onion *(diced)*
1 rib celery *(diced)*
2 bay leaves
1 sprig thyme
2 garlic cloves *(smashed)*
4 large leeks *(sliced in circles)*
½ cup white wine
½ cup cream
6 Tbs red wine vinaigrette *(see pg. 180)*

Add the lentils, water, carrot, onion, celery, thyme, bay leaf, and garlic together in a medium-sized pot. Bring the lentils to a boil, turn down, and lightly simmer them for 45 minutes, or until the lentils are fully cooked through. Keep the lentils in this liquid until serving.

Warm 2 tablespoons of butter in a medium skillet and add in the leeks. Cook them until they are soft, but without adding any color. Deglaze with the white wine and completely reduce. Then add in the cream and reduce by half. Season the leeks with salt and pepper.

Heat a steel or cast iron fish skillet over a medium high flame. Season the skate with sea salt and freshly cracked coriander. Add 2 tablespoons of the oil to the hot pan and carefully place the fish in the pan. Do not overcrowd your frying pan. If there is not an inch of space on each side of the fish, you might have to cook in two pans. Cook the fish for 1 minute on the stove top. Add in 6 tablespoons of butter and baste the skate with the melting butter. When the skate has cooked for 4 minutes, flip the skate over for an additional 2 minutes. Remove the fish from the pan and serve it with the coriander seared side facing up.

PREP **50 MINUTES**
COOK **15 MINUTES**
SERVES **6**

To serve, place one skate wing on each of the warm dinner plates. Spoon on a couple of table-spoons of the lentils and then the leeks. Drizzle the red wine vinaigrette around the plate.

GREY SOLE ROULADES
with spinach, peppers, and saffron mussel sauce

12 grey sole fillets (4 oz each)
1 lb baby spinach
6 oz roasted piquillo pepper
2 cups mussel stock
48 reserved mussels from stock
6 Tbs butter
2 lemons
4 oz cream

SAFFRON MUSSEL SAUCE:
2 cups fish stock (see pg. 169)
1 pinch saffron
48 mussels (roughly 3 pounds)
½ cup white wine

Make sure the skin is removed from the sole. Place the fillet on a work surface, skin side up. Season the fillet with salt and pepper. Place equal pieces of the red pepper flesh on the sole. In a sauté pan, wilt 1 tablespoon of butter with the baby spinach, salt and pepper. Cool the spinach before using in the roulade. Lay the spinach on top of the pepper and sole. Roll up the roulade starting at the thinner end. Stick a toothpick through the center of the fish to hold the shape of the roulade.

Bring the wine and fish stock to a boil. Add in the mussels and cook them covered for 8 minutes. Strain the liquid and reserve for cooking the fish. Pick out the mussels and reserve the meat for finalizing the sauce.

Rub a roasting pan with 2 tablespoons of butter and place the roulades in the pan. Bring the mussel stock to a boil, pour it around the fish and roast in the oven at 350 degrees for 10 minutes. Quickly remove the fish to a warm plate to slow down the cooking. Reduce the pan's liquid by half and add the cream, reserved mussels, and the last 2 tablespoons butter and whisk to incorporate. Season with the juice from the lemons, salt, and pepper.

To serve, remove the toothpicks from the sole and slice them in half to expose the filling. Arrange equal portions on all of the plates. Spoon the sauce over and around the fish.

PREP 30 MINUTES
COOK 15 MINUTES
SERVES 6

DOVER SOLE

with honshemeji mushrooms, white asparagus, napa cabbage, and washington truffle sauce

6 whole Dover sole (1 lb each)

24 young white asparagus

6 Tbs grape seed oil

1 head Napa cabbage

1 lb pea sprouts

10 oz Honshemeji mushroom

4 cups fish stock (see pg. 169)

2 cups white wine

13 Tbs unsalted butter

2 Tbs black truffle butter
(source: gourmet store)

1 lemon

1 small black truffle

Peel the white asparagus and trim off the tough end. Tie the asparagus in a little bundle with some kitchen twine so they do not get damaged in the boiling water. Place the asparagus in a large pot of salted boiling water and make sure not to overcrowd the pot. Get an ice bath ready for the asparagus while they are cooking. Cook it for 2 minutes, and test a bite. Continue this process until the asparagus is cooked to your liking. Immediately place the asparagus in the ice bath to stop the cooking. Keep the asparagus refrigerated until you need to warm them.

Slice the head of Napa cabbage in half lengthwise. Lay it down on the cut side to keep the head stable for slicing. Start at the green end and thinly slice the cabbage until you get about 2 inches from the root. I like the fresh pea flavor the sprouts add to the cabbage in this dish. If you cannot find pea sprouts you could easily substitute sugar snap peas. Blanch those like the asparagus before putting them in with the cabbage.

Melt two tablespoons of butter in a sauté pan until it begins to bubble. Add the cabbage and sauté for 1 full minute. Stir the pan so you do not add color to the cabbage. Deglaze with 2 cups of white wine. Cook the wine until it is almost gone. Add the pea sprouts at this time along with the 4 cups of fish stock and cook for 1 more minute. Season the cabbage with salt and white pepper. Drain the liquid from the cabbage through a strainer into a small sauce pot. Cover the cabbage in the sauté pan and keep off the heat on a warm part of the stove. Trim the mushrooms so they are individually removed from the root. Keep the root for the fish stock in this recipe. Place the mushrooms in the stock pot with the cabbage juices. Reduce this mixture by two-thirds. Whisk in 2 tablespoons of black truffle butter and 3 tablespoons of unsalted butter. Season the sauce with salt and pepper and the juice of the lemon. Keep warm until the fish is ready.

Heat a large cast iron or steel sauté skillet over a medium high flame. When you see the pan is hot, add the grape seed oil. Season the fish with salt and pepper. In a big pan you might be able to sauté 2 fish at a time. Place the fish in the pan and sauté for 2 minutes. Flip the fish over and add 1 tablespoon of butter to the pan. Sauté for an additional 4 minutes while basting the fish with the melted and browning butter. You baste by tilting the skillet slightly and spooning the butter over the top of the fish. If the butter looks like it is going to burn, turn the heat down. Remove the fish when you can see the flesh is separating slightly from the bone. Place it on a baking pan and keep it in a warm oven while you repeat the process for the other fish. Clean the skillet when the fish are done and melt the last 2 tablespoons of butter with the asparagus.

To serve, place a pile of the warm cabbage and pea sprouts on six plates. Equally divide the asparagus and place next to the cabbage. Lay the cooked fish over the asparagus and prop the tail against the pile of cabbage. Spoon the sauce with the mushrooms over the fish. With a truffle shaver or sharp peeler, shave thin slices of the fresh truffle over the fish.

PREP 30 MINUTES

COOK 15 MINUTES

SERVES 6

BLACK TRUMPET CRUSTED HALIBUT

with zucchini and thyme sauce

6 thick halibut fillets *(7 oz each)*
3 Tbs butter
1 cup white wine
1 lemon
2 cloves garlic *(smashed)*

1 lb black trumpet mushrooms
4 oz soft butter
4 Tbs brioche crumbs
1 Tbs fresh horseradish

6 small zucchini

THYME SAUCE:
1 cup veal stock *(see pg. 169)*
1 Tbs butter *(cold)*
4 sprigs thyme

Clean the mushrooms very well to remove any stems or dirt. Black trumpets are notorious for being a dirty mushroom. Sauté them in a non-stick pan over medium high heat for 5 minutes with 1 tablespoon of butter. Season them with salt and pepper. Transfer them to a plate. Reserve half of the mushrooms to re-heat before serving. Dice the other half up as fine as you can get it. Mix the minced mushroom in a bowl with the soft butter, brioche crumbs, horseradish, salt, and pepper.

Season the halibut fillets with salt and white pepper and coat a thin layer of the mushroom crust on their tops. Take the remaining 2 tablespoons of butter for coating a baking dish. Place the halibut fillets on the buttered baking dish and add the wine, lemon, and garlic. Bake the fish in a 350 degree oven for 8 minutes. Transfer the fish to a warm plate before serving. Cut the flesh part of the zucchini into little planks and place them in the wine broth. Place the zucchini in the oven for 3 minutes.

Thyme sauce:
Reduce the veal stock by half in a saucepot over a medium high heat. Remove the sauce from the heat and whisk in the cold butter. Tear the thyme with your hands to release its flavor. Add it to the sauce and let it steep for 2 minutes. Strain and season with salt.

To serve, place the zucchini planks on each of the six plates. Place some of the warm mushroom on top of the squash. Lay the fish on the mushrooms. Spoon some of the thyme sauce around.

PREP 30 MINUTES
COOK 15 MINUTES
SERVES 6

MOIST :: MILD :: FLAKY :: GENTLE

SEAFOOD GLOSSARY

FLORIDA RED SNAPPER

True Florida red snapper are much more flavorful than their Pacific counterparts. The snapper flesh is lean and firm yet delicate. It pairs well with the sweetness of the smooth yam and raw onion flavor of the grilled scallion. The orange, cumin, and carrot in the sauce give us a light tropical feel.

BARRAMUNDI

Barramundi is new to America, but very well known in its native country, Australia. The wild fish is considered the best, but the farm raised fish of the Northern Territory has unique texture and flavor. Similar to a wild striped bass, or if you are a sportsman, the snook fish, the Barramundi has a soft texture with white flavorful meat. It is not oily, but has moist meat, which makes it compatible with either buttery or acidic pairings. I like to match the soft texture of the fish and oyster with the crunchy brittleness of the potato and the subtle flavor of cooked cucumber. The lemon in the sauce adds a mild acidity, and the thyme and garlic sprout give an earthy flavor.

BLACK BASS

Black bass is delicate with great flavor. It has sweet fine flaking meat that remains moist even when cooked through. In this recipe, I like to use the crunchy texture of the sautéed potatoes to help balance the soft texture of the fish. The beet flavor adds earthiness and spring freshness to the dish.

COD

I like the flavor of the larger Atlantic cod. This fish has light, flaky, white meat. It is best cooked almost through, but not dried out. I like to serve it with peas and pearl onions, a classic marriage, and what better with peas than ham. The freshness of the pea sprouts and the elegance of the Italian ham give us those flavors at a more refined level.

PAN ROASTED FLORIDA RED SNAPPER
with boniato puree, globe carrots, and orange cumin sauce

6 snapper fillets *(7 oz. each)*
2 bunch green onions
2 dozen baby carrots
2 Tbs extra virgin olive oil

BONIATO:

3 lbs Boniato potato
¼ lb butter
1 cup heavy cream
2 lemons

ORANGE CUMIN SAUCE:

2 cups fresh squeezed orange juice
2 cups fresh carrot juice
1 Tbs coriander seeds
3 Tbs cumin seeds
2 Tbs garlic *(chopped)*
2 shallots
1 cup chicken stock
4 Tbs butter
1 lime

PREP **40 MINUTES**
COOK **10 MINUTES**
SERVES **6**

Heat up a heavy cast iron or steel pan over a medium high flame. Add a couple of tablespoons of olive oil to the pan and let the oil get hot. Season the fish with salt and pepper. Place the snapper fillets in the pan with the skin side down. Sauté for 2 minutes and turn the heat down to medium. Cook the fish for an additional 4 minutes. Flip the fish over for the last minute of cooking. The snapper will continue to cook as it makes its trip to the table or while it waits to be enjoyed.

Plunge the green onions in salted boiling water for 20 seconds and then transfer them to a bowl with ice water. Do the same with the peeled baby carrots, but you will need to cook them for a minute longer than the green onions. When you are ready to serve the dish, you can warm them up in a sauté pan with 2 tablespoons of olive oil, salt and pepper.

Peel and place the boniato in salted water with the juice of one lemon. Boil the potato until it is tender. Immediately strain the potato and pass it through a sieve or simply smash. Bring the cream to a boil. Fold the cold butter into the warm potato until it has incorporated. Add the boiling cream to the potato mixture and season with salt and pepper. Finish with a squeeze of fresh lemon juice.

In a saucepan over medium heat, lightly sauté the chopped shallots and garlic. Deglaze with the orange juice and carrot juice and bring to a boil. While you are waiting, toast the cumin and coriander in a dry pan and blend into powder in a spice grinder. Add the spices to the boiling juices. Reduce the juice by half and add the chicken stock. Reduce the mixture by half again. Whisk in the butter, juice of one lime, and season with salt and pepper.

To serve, place a spoon a boniato purée on each plate. Arrange the snapper over the boniato and place the carrots and green onion around the outside of the boniato. Spoon the sauce over the vegetables.

AUSTRALIAN BARRAMUNDI

with crispy potato, cucumber, and oyster sauce

6 barramundi fillets *(7 oz. each)*
8 Tbs olive oil
4 Idaho potatoes
3 cucumbers
12 cold water oysters
6 garlic sprouts
1 Tbs fresh thyme *(chopped)*
2 cups fish cream *(see pg. 167)*
1 cup whipped cream
1 lemon

Peel and julienne the potato into thin strips. Heat a tiny cast iron sauté pan over medium high heat. Add the olive oil and place a small handful of the potato in the pan. Press the potato flat and fry for 4 minutes. Flip the potato and fry an additional 2 minutes. Repeat the process for the other 5 potato cakes. Season with salt and keep them in a warm place.

Peel and julienne the cucumber. Discard the seeded center. Blanch the garlic sprouts in boiling water for 4 minutes. Shuck the oysters and place them in a pan with their juice. Put the fish cream in with the oysters and warm them over a medium heat. Place the cucumber and the garlic sprouts in with the oysters. Bring the mixture to a boil and season with salt, pepper, thyme and lemon juice. Stir in the whipped cream.

Heat a cast iron or steel sauté pan over a medium high heat. Season the fish with salt and pepper. Put a couple of tablespoons of oil in the pan and place the fish in skin side down. Cook the fish for 2 minutes on the stove and transfer the pan to a 400 degree oven for 5 minutes. Remove the fish from the oven and flip it over on the flesh side for 30 seconds. Place the fish on a warm plate until ready to serve.

To serve, spoon a pile of the cucumbers on each plate. Place a couple of oysters and the sauce around the cucumber. Place the crispy potato on the cucumber and the fish on top of that. Lean the garlic over the fish.

PREP 50 MINUTES
COOK 15 MINUTES
SERVES 6

PROSCIUTTO-WRAPPED CODFISH
with pea greens, pearl onions, and pea sauce

6 thick codfish fillets *(7 oz. each)*
2 Tbs olive oil
6 thin sheets of shaved
   Italian prosciutto
1 lb golden pea greens
1 pint pearl onions
4 Tbs butter
1 cup green pea sauce *(see pg. 166)*
2 oz whipped cream

For this presentation you will need to get the fillets from a large codfish. Season the fish with salt and pepper and wrap it in the one of the prosciutto slices. Repeat the process for the other five fillets. Place a cast iron or steel sauté pan over a medium high heat. Add the olive oil to the pan and sauté the fish for 30 seconds on each side. Place 2 tablespoons of butter in the pan and place it in a 400 degree oven for an additional 5 minutes. Transfer the fish to a warm plate and let it rest.

Blanch the pearl onions in salted boiling water for 5 minutes. Shock them in cold water. Cut off the root end and squeeze out the clean onion.

Warm a sauté pan with the other 2 tablespoons of butter. Place the pearl onions in the pan and sauté them for 1 minute. Toss the golden pea tendrils in the pan and season with salt and pepper. Cook for 20 seconds and transfer them equally to the six serving plates. Place a warm fish in the center of each plate.

PREP 30 MINUTES
COOK 15 MINUTES
SERVES 6

Warm up the pea sauce and whisk in the cream. Spoon it around the fish.

CRISPY WHOLE FARM-RAISED STRIPED BASS

with asian sauces

3 whole	striped bass *(1 lb each)*
1 cup	corn starch
10 cups	canola or peanut oil
1 pkg	cellophane noodles
8 cups	water
4 Tbs	soy sauce
2 Tbs	sesame oil
1	lime
1	bunch green onion
1 cup	spicy chili aioli *(see pg. 176)*
1 cup	soy citrus juice *(see pg. 181)*
1 cup	black bean sauce *(see pg. 182)*

You should be able to get this fish very fresh due to the fact that it is farm-raised. Have your butcher dress it for you to fry. It needs to be gutted, scaled, gills removed, and trimmed of the side and dorsal fins. You can score the flesh of the fish to let it cook to the bone more evenly.

Heat a large deep fryer to 350 degrees. Dust the bass with cornstarch and salt and lower it carefully into the fryer. The fish will take about 10 minutes to cook through. Drain it on paper towels and season again with salt and cracked pepper.

Bring the salted water to a boil. Add the glass noodles and turn the water off. Let the noodles steep until tender. Drain the noodles and season them with the chopped green onion, sesame oil, soy sauce, and lime juice.

Place the noodles on three different serving plates. Place a crispy fish on the top of each noodle pile. Serve 1 fish per couple and give each person a small plate with the assorted dipping sauces.

PREP **30 MINUTES**
COOK **15 MINUTES**
SERVES **6**

WILD STRIPED BASS

with creamy vidalia onions and red currants

6 wild striped bass fillets *(7 oz. each)*

10 Vidalia onions
   (or substitute any sweet onion)

2 cups chicken stock *(see pg. 168)*

1 cup cream

1 pint fresh red currants
   (or substitute champagne grapes)

2 Tbs butter

6 Tbs olive oil

To make the caramelized onions heat a large heavy bottom sauté pan over a medium high heat. Slice the onions in half and peel them. Lay them flat and cut very thin slices. Add the butter to the hot pan and place the onions on top. Season the onions lightly with salt. Keep stirring the onions as they begin to wilt down. You will have to keep a close eye on this project. As the onions wilt they will release their liquid and it will evaporate. When the liquid is gone, the onions' sugar will get hotter and begin to caramelize. When the onions begin to turn a dark brown, add in 1/4 cup of water. Stir the onions around and scrape the bottom of the pan. Now the water will evaporate and the onions will turn brown once again. Add water again and repeat this process until the onion mixture is completely dark brown. Do not let the mixture burn or it will ruin the taste of the garnish. Now that the onions are dark brown, add the chicken stock. Reduce the chicken stock by 1/3 and then add the cream. When the mixture comes back to a boil, turn it off. With a slotted spoon, take out a spoon of onions for each plate. Put the rest of the onions and sauce in a blender. Blend and strain the sauce and season with salt and pepper. Warm the sauce back up in a pan with the red currants. Keep it warm until the fish are ready.

Heat a cast iron or steel sauté pan over a medium high heat. Add the oil and let it get very hot. Season the fish with sea salt and cracked pepper. Sauté the fish skin side down for 3 minutes. Transfer the pan to a 350 degree oven for 4 more minutes. Remove the pan from the oven and flip the fillet. Let the fish cook for 20 more seconds in the pan with no flame. Transfer to a warm plate.

Place the spoon of onions on each warm serving plate. Place the fish on top of the onions. Spoon the sauce around.

PREP 30 MINUTES
COOK 10 MINUTES
SERVES 6

PAN-ROASTED BLACK BASS

with potato hash and organic beet cream

6 black bass fillets *(7 oz. each)*

3 jumbo Yukon gold potatoes

2 Tbs olive oil

1 dozen baby beets *(white, red, or gold)*

2 Tbs butter

1 lemon *(juiced)*

1 cup organic beet cream *(see pg. 166)*

I like to have the fishmonger leave the skin on these fillets to help to protect the flesh of the fish during frying. Make small incisions in the skin of the fish to help prevent it from curling during the cooking process. You can also press it flat with a spatula.

Heat a cast iron or steel fish skillet over a medium high heat. Add the grape seed oil and let it get hot. Carefully add the fish to the pan skin side down. Sauté the fish for 4 minutes on one side and flip it over for an additional 2 minutes. Remove the fish to a warm plate to rest.

Peel and dice the potatoes into small cubes and keep them in cold water until needed. Get a non stick sauté pan hot over a medium high heat. Add the olive oil to the pan. Drain the potatoes of any water and add them to the hot oil. Season the potatoes with salt and pepper while cooking. Toss the pan and cook for 5 minutes. The potatoes should be golden brown and cooked throughout.

Blanch the baby beets in salted boiling water for 10 minutes. Remove the skin and cut the beets in half. Transfer them to a sauté pan with the butter and cook for an additional 2 minutes over a medium heat. Season the beets with salt, pepper, and lemon juice.

Warm the beet cream in a small sauce pot and keep hot.

To serve, place equal portions of the potatoes on six plates. Place the fish fillet on top of the potatoes. Divide the baby beets between the dishes. Spoon the warm beet cream around the plates.

PREP **30 MINUTES**

COOK **15 MINUTES**

SERVES **6**

TENDER :: BUTTERY :: SWEET :: SUCCULENT

oyster › pg. 90

SEAFOOD GLOSSARY

SOFT-SHELL CRAB

Eastern shore soft-shells have a special place in my heart. I love the chewy texture of the shell with the sweetness of the meat. It has natural balance. I serve it with the creaminess of goat cheese polenta, basically, a spruced up southern grits. The red pepper sauce gives you the acidic and spicy flavor, and the baby radish give you a garden freshness.

STONE CRAB

Florida stone crabs are the premier delicacy of our region. They are sweet and moist with incredible crab flavor. They have a good amount of fat for a crab of warm waters. I mostly serve the stone crab simply using a balancing sauce like spicy honey mustard or acidic avocado purée. The crab will however hold up to strong flavor combinations.

GOLDEN CRAB

The Florida golden crab was discovered when fish traps fell off the continental shelf into very deep waters. They came back up with a large golden crab. Its flavor is mild and not as sweet as the popular stone crab, but when paired with buttery flavors, it can be a very tasty creature. I like to give it more excitement by adding the spice of the pepper and the herbal flavors of cilantro and parsley. The acidity of the lime and vinegar help to cut the large amount of butter added to the dish. Roasting the crab with the butter gives it a nice nutty flavor and mellows the strength of the onion and pepper.

MUSSEL

Personally, I am fond of the smaller varieties of the mussel family. I like to serve the small bouchot mussel from Maine. The Prince Edward Island (PEI) is larger than the baby Maine mussel, the Mediterranean is even larger, and the largest is the New Zealand green lip. Feel free to substitute your favorite. Mussels hold up well to spicy and salty flavors. I like to use the Asian flavors of ginger and lemongrass with this dish. Chinese chili adds the spiciness and lemon brings the acidity to cut the buttery flavor of the broth. I enjoy the broth of the mussels as much as the mussels themselves, so I always make plenty of liquid for them.

NANTUCKET SCALLOP

The sweeter more delicate version of the sea scallop is a true treat. I like the mix of the salty sweet of the scallop and the fruity sweet of the pear. The velvety celery flavor is the mild undertone between the two. The shell of the fresh scallop makes a perfect container for this soup shot appetizer.

SEA SCALLOP

Live sea scallops are an amazing experience. Everything from the impressive shell to the beauty of its simplicity. When you clean them, the edible mussel stands out like a shining silver dollar. You have found your treasure! Gently seared to accent its sweetness, and paired with the light earthiness of fennel, it is a treasure that will not last long. The salty pancetta and parsley give a nice balance of meaty and herbal flavor.

OYSTER

Growing up near the water I really came to love the fresh saltiness of raw oysters. My favorite are the smaller varieties with firm texture, bright saltiness, and cold cucumber flavor. The tarragon mignonette has a strong acidity which gives the oyster a nice boost. The shallots add a touch of crunchiness to this great ocean treat.

CHESAPEAKE SOFT SHELL CRAB

with soft polenta, baby radishes, and sweet pepper sauce

6	Chesapeake soft shell blue crabs
6 cups	canola oil
2 bunch	baby radishes
2 Tbs	butter
1 Tbs	water
1 Tbs	sugar
1 cup	flour
1 cup	soda water
pinch	ginger powder
pinch	baking soda
4 oz	polenta
3 cups	chicken stock *(see pg. 168)*
2 oz	butter
3 oz	goat cheese
2 oz	crème fraiche
1	lemon
1 cup	sweet pepper sauce *(see pg. 170)*

Whisk the flour, ginger, baking soda, soda water and salt. Chill the tempura batter in the refrigerator until needed. Bring the chicken stock to a boil in a large sauce pot. Whisk in the polenta and turn the heat down to a slow bubble. Stir the polenta frequently over the next 40 minutes. Whisk in the butter, crème fraiche, and goat cheese until the polenta has a smooth consistency. Season with salt, pepper, and the lemon juice.

Ask the fishmonger to clean the crabs if you do not know how. They should remove the gills, eyes, and apron. Heat the oil in a small deep fryer to 350 degrees. Dust the crabs in some flour and then into the tempura batter. Fry the crabs whole for 3 minutes. Drain them on a paper towel and season with sea salt.

Place the baby radishes with the sugar, butter, and water in a medium sauté pan. Season them with salt and pepper. Cook the radishes over medium high heat until the water has evaporated. If the radishes are not completely cooked, just add more water. They should be nicely glazed at this time.

To serve, place a large spoon of the polenta on six plates. Place one crab over each pile of polenta. Lay the baby radishes next to the crab and drizzle the pepper sauce around.

PREP **60 MINUTES**
COOK **15 MINUTES**
SERVES **6**

BABY MAINE MUSSELS
with ginger lemongrass broth

3 lbs black mussels

2 inch piece of ginger root

1 stalk lemongrass

1 Tbs Chinese sambal chili paste
(Asian grocer)

2 Tbs chopped garlic

2 Tbs olive oil

1 cup dry white wine

1 cup fish stock

1 bunch cilantro

2 lemons

¼ lb butter

Clean the mussels in cold water removing anything foreign from the shells. To check for dead mussels, tap them on the sink and notice if they try to close. If they do not budge and remain wide open, discard them. Store mussels in the refrigerator covered with a damp towel, but never leave them submerged in water for long periods of time.

Peel the ginger root and slice it into thin slices. Lay the slices flat and slice them thin again to make fine thin strands. Peel the tough outer leaves off of the lemongrass. Cut the stalk into 1-inch sticks. Lightly smash the sticks to let the lemongrass release its flavor.

Heat up a large sauté pan with the olive oil over a medium high heat. Add the ginger, lemongrass, chili paste, and garlic and sauté for 1 minute. Add the mussels and stir the pan while cooking for an additional minute. Deglaze the pan with the white wine. Add the fish stock and cover the dish with a lid and cook the mussels for 4 minutes. Remove the lid and let the sauce reduce with the mussels. Add the butter and stir it into the broth. Season the broth with salt and pepper to taste. When the 2 cups of liquid has reduced by half, add the juice from the lemons and the leaves of the cilantro.

Pour the mussels and the broth into individual serving bowls.

PREP 10 MINUTES

COOK 10 MINUTES

SERVES 6

FLORIDA STONE CRAB

with four variations

6 jumbo Florida stone crabs

METHOD ONE:

12 oz spicy honey mustard aioli
(see pg. 175)

1 lime

METHOD TWO:

1 large beet

1 cup grape seed oil

3 Tbs curry apple aioli *(see pg. 176)*

2 Tbs chopped chives

1 lemon

METHOD THREE:

2 ripe avocados

1 Tbs sesame oil

1 lime

1 Tbs toasted sesame seeds

METHOD FOUR:

3 Tbs garlic aioli *(see pg. 173)*

1 oz cilantro sprouts

1 lemon

1 large watermelon radish

1 tsp salt

1 cup pickling juice *(see pg. 170)*

PREP 20 MINUTES

COOK 5 MINUTES

SERVES 6

You need at least 1 jumbo crab claw per person for any of the methods.

METHOD ONE: This is the purist method where the crab is serve just cracked with a side of spicy mustard sauce and a wedge of lime.

METHOD TWO: Peel and slice the large beets into very thin circles. Heat the grape seed oil in a small frying pan and add the beet slices. Fry the beet chips until crispy, but before they turn brown. Drain them on a paper towel and season with sea salt. Pick all the meat from the crab claws and mix it in a bowl with the curry aioli, chives, and juice from the lemon. Adjust the seasoning with salt and pepper. On 6 individual plates, serve equal portions of the crab meat mixture and beet chips.

METHOD THREE: Crack the claws of the crabs leaving the pincher part intact. Pick all the knuckle meat and reserve. Slice the avocados in half and remove the seed. Scoop out the flesh and smash it in a bowl with the sesame oil, lime juice, salt and pepper. Mix in the sesame seeds and the knuckle meat at the end. Spoon out equal portions of the avocado dip on 6 plates and prop 1 claw in each of the mounds of avocado.

METHOD FOUR: Peel and slice the watermelon radish in thin slices. Place them in a bowl and cover the radish with the pickling juice and salt. Let the radish marinate for 1 hour, then drain the pickling juice. Pick the meat from all the crabs and mix it in a bowl with the garlic aioli, cilantro sprouts, lemon juice, salt and pepper. In a small circular mold, arrange the drained slices of radish. Spoon the crab mixture in the center of the radish circles. Remove the mold and serve.

SOUP SHOTS OF NANTUCKET SCALLOPS

with asian pear and celery root soup

FOR SOUP:

1 bulb	celery root
1	small Yukon gold potato
2	leeks
1	Asian pear
2	shallots
2 Tbs	butter
1 cup	dry white wine
8 cups	chicken stock *(see pg. 168)*
1 cup	cream
1	lemon
18	live Nantucket bay scallops
1 cup	dry white wine
4 Tbs	butter
2	leeks
1	lemon
¼ cup	parsley purée *(see pg. 182)*

PREP 50 MINUTES

COOK 15 MINUTES

SERVES 6

For the soup, you need to chop the shallots. Then clean and cut the leeks in rounds. Peel and dice the celery root, potato, and pear. Nothing needs to be cut perfectly since it will all get puréed later in the dish. Start by melting the butter in a stainless steel stock pot over a medium heat. Add the shallots and leeks and cook for 2 minutes. Then add the pear and cook for 1 minute more. Toss in the celery root, potato, and the white wine and cook until the wine is gone. Season lightly with salt and white pepper. Add the chicken stock and bring the soup to a boil. Turn down the heat to simmer until the potatoes are cooked (roughly 15 minutes). Add the cream and let it cook for 3 minutes. Take the soup off the heat and let it cool for 10 minutes. Purée the soup in a blender. Only fill your blender halfway with soup and be careful it is not on the highest setting when you turn it on. Strain the puréed soup and place it back in a sauce pot to keep it warm. Adjust the seasoning with fresh lemon juice, salt and pepper.

If you find fresh scallops, you clean them by running a knife down the flat sided shell through the small opening in the side of the connected end. This will cut the mussel that holds the shells together. You will now remove and discard the flat shell. Pull off and discard any of the body of the scallop leaving the clean white mussel intact with the shell. If you notice a smooth orange sack next to the mussel, you might want to leave it attached. This is the egg sack and is very tasty. If you do not like that sort of thing, simply discard it. Rinse the scallop with the shell under clean cold water to remove any sand or debris. Continue this process with the rest of the scallops. If you cannot get live scallops, you can use the already shucked ones and serve the soup in a bowl.

Heat a sauté pan with the 4 tablespoons of butter. Meanwhile, cut the leeks into perfect 1/8-inch rounds. Thoroughly wash the leeks in cold water to remove any dirt. Sauté them with the butter over a medium heat for 4 minutes. Lay the scallops on a sheet pan and spoon a tablespoon of the cooked leeks over the scallop. Place a teaspoon of white wine and a couple of drops of lemon on each of the scallops. Season them with salt and pepper and place them in a 350 degree oven for 8 minutes.

When you remove the scallops from the oven, transfer them to a serving tray covered in coarse salt. Prop the shells so that they are level. Spoon 2 tablespoons of soup over each of the scallops and finish them with a dot of parsley purée.

MAINE DIVER SEA SCALLOPS
with fennel confit, crispy pancetta, and parsley sauce

6 live sea scallops
2 fennel bulbs
¼ cup extra virgin olive oil
2 stars anise
6 thin slices of pancetta
6 Tbs parsley oil *(see p. 182)*

Cut the fennel bulbs in half from top to bottom. Cut out the root from the bottom. Lay the fennel bulbs down on the flat side and shave them into thin slices. Place them in a sauce pan with the virgin olive oil, star anise, and some course sea salt. Cook the fennel on the lowest temperature of your stove top for 30 minutes. Lay the slices of pancetta on a sheet pan and bake in the oven for 10 minutes at 350 degrees.

To clean the scallops, insert a long thin sharp knife down the inside of the flat shell to cut the scallop mussel from one side of the shell. Now you will be able to separate the shells. Discard the flat shell. Pull the scallop body away from the white mussel that keeps the shell together. If you notice a bright orange egg sack, you can leave that to cook with the scallop. Slice the scallop out of the bottom shell and keep the shell for presentation. Heat a cast iron skillet or steel pan over medium high heat. Place a spoonful of the fennel oil from the cooked fennel in the sauté pan.

Season the scallops with salt and pepper and place them in the pan. Sauté the scallops 2 minutes on each side. Transfer the scallops to a warm plate.

To serve, place a folded napkin on each of the six plates. Warm the shells of the scallop in the oven and place them on the napkins. Spoon some of the fennel on each shell and top it with the scallop. Place a tablespoon of the parsley oil around each scallop. Stick the crispy pancetta on the side of each shell.

PREP **45 MINUTES**
COOK **15 MINUTES**
SERVES **6**

FLORIDA GOLDEN CRABS
with jalapeño garlic butter

3 whole golden crabs
3 gal court bouillon *(see pg. 168)*
1 lb butter
2 Tbs garlic confit *(see pg. 172)*
6 jalapeño peppers
6 shallots
2 Tbs white vinegar
2 limes
4 Tbs olive oil
1 bunch cilantro
1 bunch parsley

Bring the court bouillon to a boil in a large stock pot. Place the crabs in the pot and cook them for 10 minutes. Take them off the heat and let the crabs cool in the liquid. Break off the shell and discard with the guts and gills. Break the body into quarters and refrigerate until needed.

Finely dice the peppers and shallots. Mix them with the garlic, vinegar, limes, olive oil, chopped cilantro and chopped parsley. In a roasting pan, place the crab quarters and butter. Roast in the oven for 3 minutes at 350 degrees. Baste the crabs with the butter and add in the pepper mixture. Bake for an additional 6 minutes, basting every couple of minutes. Remove the crabs and place equal portions on the six serving plates. This is a messy dinner and should be enjoyed in a more casual environment.

Serve a salad that is acidic and fresh tasting. Tomato, cucumber, or lettuces would all be great. Keep the dressing lighter and lemony, not creamy.

PREP 50 MINUTES
COOK 15 MINUTES
SERVES 6

CHILLED PACIFIC OYSTERS
with tarragon champagne mignonette

3 dozen	cold water oysters
2	shallots
2 Tbs	chopped tarragon
2 tsp	sea salt
2 Tbs	fresh ground black pepper
1 cup	Champagne vinegar
1	lemon

We buy all of our oysters from cold water locations. I get most of them from the Pacific Northwest and some from New England. Look for clean oysters that feel heavy. The key to opening the oyster is popping the joint at the back where the two shells connect. Then the only thing holding them together is the mussel of the oyster. On a clean surface with a wet towel as a base, position the oyster with the flatter shell facing up. Gently twist the oyster knife in the groove at the back of oyster. You only want to pop the connection open. Do not try to jam the knife into the oyster. When the joint is popped, scrape the oyster knife along the upper right edge of the shell to cut the connector mussel. The oyster shells will now be separated. You will now see the oyster as it is only connected to one of the shells. Carefully, scrape the other mussel to free the oyster from the shell. Be careful not to spill all the juices in the shell. Place the oyster on a bed of ice in a pan. Continue to open the rest of the oysters. By the time you get to the last one, you should have the hang of it.

Mince the shallots with a sharp knife. You can use a food processor for garlic, but never use it to mince shallots. Add the shallots to a bowl and add the vinegar, sea salt, ground pepper, and tarragon. Let the mignonette chill in the refrigerator for 30 minutes to let the flavors meld.

To serve, arrange the oysters on six individual bowl plates with ice. It helps to put a napkin in the bowl so the ice does not slide around when it starts to melt. Put some of the mignonette in individual serving cups for each plate. Garnish the plates with wedge of lemon and serve while very cold.

PREP 10 MINUTES
COOK 5 MINUTES
SERVES 6

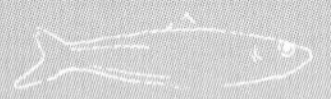

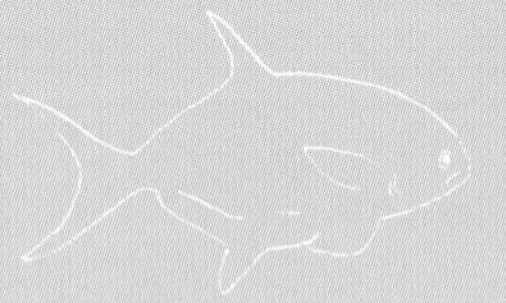

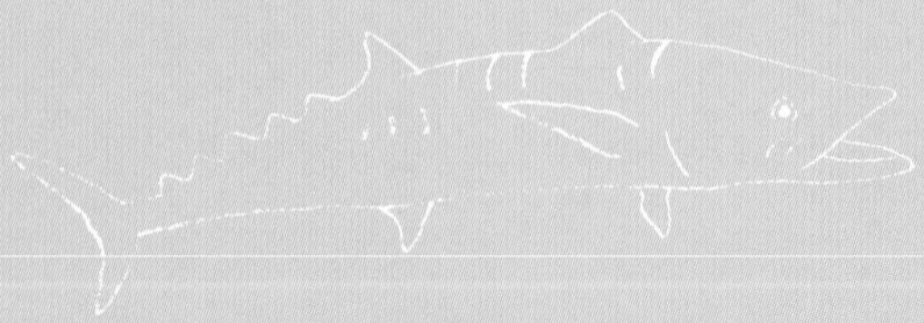

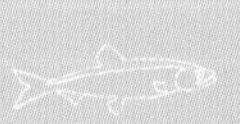

SILKY :: SMOOTH :: FLAVORFUL :: INTENSE

SEAFOOD GLOSSARY

CHAR

Arctic char is a very cold water marriage between a trout and a salmon. The meat is very fatty and pink and has great flavor. It pairs well with the salty flavor of the sausage and the acidic flavor of the mustard sauce. The potatoes add a gentle earthy tone and the sauerkraut brings more acidity to refresh the buttery fish.

SALMON

Salmon is a fatty fish that can get dry if it is overcooked. It has strong flavor that is best balanced with high acidity. The endive is bitter in nature, and we balance it with sugar during the cooking process. The bittersweet result is a great balance with the strength of the salmon. No matter where you work, there is something to learn in every kitchen. Brussels sprout stoemp is one I picked up along the way. This rural style of root vegetable preparation has always intrigued me. I use it to add smooth earthiness which gives contrast to the chewy salmon and endive. The red wine shallots give the high acidity needed to balance all the fattiness of the dish.

SALMON TARTAR

Salmon tartar is a great use for the oily belly meat. The flavor of the belly when cooked is more intense than the subtle butteriness you get when it's raw. The pickled daikon gives some sweet freshness to the dish, the caviar gives us some saltiness, and the acidic yuzu aioli adds the smooth flavor boost the dish needs. The mache adds a nice leafy texture element.

SARDINE

Sardines are small fish with a powerful flavor. You need freshness and acidity to balance their oily strong flavor. The light texture of the tomatoes are a good balance with the sardine's delicate meat. The smooth creaminess of the eggplant and its gentle bitterness help the lemon vinaigrette to balance the strength of such a little fish.

KINGFISH

Kingfish can become a bit dry if it is cooked through. Even though it is considered an oily fish, it has a very lean fillet that matches well with acidity. The earthy flavor of the garlic and yucca give the dish some soft textures to balance the stronger textures of the fish and greens.

POMPANO

Pompano is a thin, fast, silvery fish we get off the coast of Florida. The fillets are thin, white, and firm. They have a robust flavor that holds up to strong pairings. I like to grill this fish whole to give it that beach campfire appeal. Its flavor and oiliness do well with the strong flavor of open fire. I like to pair it with an acidic salad to balance its intensity. The salad brings in all dimensions of flavor and texture. The fresh heart of palm gives us a crunchy nuttiness, and the avocado gives us smooth creaminess. The pickled onion gives us an earthiness. The arugula gives us that spicy pepper flavor and the passion fruit vinaigrette bring it all together with a brightness that cleanses the palate.

SMELT

Smelt are small fish that are similar to Herring. They are great fried and left on the bone. The tiny edible bones add a great crunchiness to the dish. The fish has very white lightly flavored meat. Its taste reminds me of summer fish fries growing up on the Chesapeake. I like to serve it with a dressed up version of coleslaw and creamy aioli to balance the crunchy texture of the fish and the chew of the salad.

BROILED SARDINES

with eggplant caviar, heirloom tomatoes, and basil oil

6 fresh whole sardines

4 medium size farm fresh tomatoes

6 Japanese purple eggplant

6 tsp basil oil *(see pg. 174)*

2 Tbs garlic confit *(see pg. 172)*

1 tsp horseradish

12 Tbs olive oil

1 bunch basil

6 Tbs lemon vinaigrette *(see pg. 177)*

I choose to use the Japanese eggplant in this recipe due to the lack of bitterness in this variety. You could use Italian eggplant, but you will need to salt them first to remove some of the bitterness from the skin and seeds. Slice the eggplant lengthwise and place them cut side up in a baking dish. Score the flesh of the eggplant with a small knife. Drizzle the eggplant with olive oil, salt and pepper. Cover the eggplant with foil and roast them in a 350 degree oven for 15 minutes. If you are using larger eggplant it might take longer. The flesh of the eggplant should be cooked through and soft. After they are cool, you use a spoon to scoop out all of the flesh (caviar) from the skin. Discard the skin. Purée the eggplant in a small food processor with the basil oil, garlic, and horseradish. Season the mixture with salt and white pepper to taste. This can be served at room temperature, but refrigerate for over a couple of hours if you do not need it.

Have your fishmonger cut the whole sardines in fillets if you are uncomfortable attempting that at home. If you want to try it, the first thing you will have to do is remove the scales. Simply run the fish under cold water and pull the scales off with your fingers. They are large and easy to remove. Then pat the fish dry with a paper towel. With a small knife, Cut the fish to remove the head. With your fingers, spread the fish apart from the belly and pull the center bone out of the fillets. If you are gentle, you can remove the main center bone and it will hold on to all the little bones in the belly. Trim the fish of the fins and season with olive oil, salt and pepper. Keep chilled until ready to broil.

Cut the root end of the tomato out and score the other end of the tomato with a small knife. Plunge the tomatoes into boiling water for 10 seconds and shock them quickly in ice cold water. Remove the skin from the tomatoes and slice them to make 6 slices per tomato. Lay them flat on a large sheet pan and drizzle them all with olive oil, salt and pepper.

Set the broiler of your stove to the highest temperature. Place the seasoned sardines skin side up on a sheet pan and broil them for 2 minutes. They only need to be cooked on one side.

To serve, fan equal portions of the tomatoes on six plates. Spoon a couple of tablespoons of the eggplant on each plate and place the warm fish on top. Drizzle the fish and tomatoes with the lemon vinaigrette. Drizzle around a teaspoon of basil oil.

PREP **40 MINUTES**

COOK **10 MINUTES**

SERVES **6**

SEARED KINGFISH
with steamed yucca and green olive salsa

6	kingfish fillets *(7 oz. each)*
6 Tbs	olive oil
1 lb	spicy braising greens
2 lb	yucca root
2	lemon
2 Tbs	garlic confit *(see pg. 172)*
1 cup	water *(or reserved cooking liquid)*
2 Tbs	butter
12 Tbs	green olive vinaigrette *(see pg. 178)*

Peel and slice the yucca in half. Place them in a pot with cold water to cover. Season the water with salt and the juice of one lemon. Bring the water to a boil and turn down the heat to simmer the yucca until its cooked through (roughly 20 minutes.) Strain the yucca and cut the halves into stick like shapes. To warm the yucca, add the water, garlic confit, and 1 tablespoon of butter to a small pan over medium heat. When the water has evaporated, the yucca will be hot and coated with a smooth sauce of garlic and butter. Season the yucca with the juice of the last lemon, salt and pepper.

Heat a cast iron or steel sauté pan over medium high heat. Add the olive oil and let it get hot. Season the fish with salt and pepper. Place the fish skin side down in the frying pan and sauté for 1 minute. Place the whole pan in the oven at 400 degrees for an additional 4 minutes. Remove the fish from the pan and keep in a warm place to let the juices rest.

In a Teflon sauté pan, heat up the last 2 tablespoons of olive oil with 1 tablespoon of butter over a medium high heat. Add the braising greens and sauté for 3 minutes. Season the greens with salt and pepper.

Place the greens on one end of the plate and the yucca on the other end. Place the fish on the greens and the olive vinaigrette over the yucca.

PREP **45 MINUTES**
COOK **20 MINUTES**
SERVES **6**

WHOLE WOOD GRILLED POMPANO
with hearts of palm salad and passion fruit sauce

3 whole	pompano (*2 lb plus*)
6 Tbs	olive oil
3 whole	passion fruit
2	limes
1 lb	baby arugula
2 stalks	fresh hearts of palm
1	avocado
1	lime
2	red onions
½ cup	pickling juice
¼ cup	lemon vinaigrette (*see pg. 177*)
½ cup	passion fruit sauce (*see pg. 179*)

A wood fire will always give you the best flavor, but you can use your gas grill just the same. Get the grill very hot and clean and oil your grill rack. Make deep cross cuts in the flesh of the pompano to allow the thicker parts of the flesh to cook faster. Rub the fish with the olive oil and season with salt and pepper. Grill the pompano 5 minutes on each side and transfer to a warm platter. Cut the passion fruit in half and squeeze the pulp from inside over the fish. Squeeze the juice of one fresh lime over each fish.

Slice the heart of palm into 1/8 inch circles and mix with the arugula. Thinly slice the red onion and marinate it in the pickling juice for at least 20 minutes. Slice the avocado and squeeze with the lime juice. Toss the pickled onions, avocado, and the lemon vinaigrette with the arugula and heart of palm. Re-season the salad with salt and pepper.

Place the salad equally on three platters. Place a fish on top of the salads. Pour the passion fruit sauce around the three platters.

PREP **60 MINUTES**
COOK **40 MINUTES**
SERVES **6**

FRIED SMELT
with savoy cabbage salad and white truffle aioli

30	small smelt
4 cups	canola oil
1 head	Savoy cabbage
2	carrots
1 bunch	cilantro
1 lb	yellow wax beans
1 lb	baby green beans
1 lb	cranberry beans
1 cup	flour
1 cup	lemon vinaigrette *(see pg. 177)*
1 cup	white truffle aioli *(see pg. 173)*
2 Tbs	orange tobiko
	(source: Japanese grocer)

Usually the smelt will come head off and gutted. The bones in the smelt are small and chew very easily when fried. Heat the canola oil in a small deep fryer. Mix the flour with some salt and white pepper. Dust the smelt with the flour and fry them in the hot oil until golden and crispy. They take about 4 minutes to completely cook.

Meanwhile, blanch the beans in salted boiling water for 2 minutes. Immediately transfer the beans to an ice bath to retain the nice color of the beans. Slice the cabbage in half and remove the large root. Shave the cabbage as thin as you can. Peel and julienne the carrot and add it to a bowl with the cabbage. Pick the leaves from the cilantro sprigs and place them in the bowl as well. Put the cooked and chilled beans in with the cabbage. Add the lemon vinaigrette and toss. Season the cabbage with 2 tablespoons of the white truffle aioli and the lemon vinaigrette.

Place the cabbage salad on six plates and arrange 5 of the smelt on each plate against the salad. Mix the tobiko with the aioli and spoon some on each plate.

PREP **30 MINUTES**
COOK **15 MINUTES**
SERVES **6**

CRISPY WILD KING SALMON

with brussels sprout potatoes, caramelized endive, and red wine shallot sauce

6 fillets of salmon
(7 oz. each, with skin on)
3 Tbs grape seed oil
3 endives
6 Tbs butter
1 Tbs sugar
¼ cup chicken stock *(see pg. 168)*
1 lemon *(juiced)*
2 pints Brussels sprouts
2 lb Yukon potatoes
1 cup cream
1 cup red wine shallot sauce

FOR RED WINE SHALLOT SAUCE:
4 shallots *(minced)*
1 cup red wine
¼ lb butter
1 Tbs sherry vinegar

PREP **50 MINUTES**
COOK **15 MINUTES**
SERVES **6**

To cook the potatoes: peel and chop the potatoes into small cubes. Clean and put 1 pint of baby Brussels sprouts on top of the potatoes in a small sauce pot. Put a good pinch of salt on the mixture and put enough water to only come up to just under the level of the potatoes. Cook the potatoes uncovered over a medium high heat. The water will quickly evaporate and leave the potatoes cooked and the sprouts steamed. Carefully watch the pot when the water is almost gone. Smash the mixture with a potato press right in the pot. Add 2 tablespoons of butter and the cream. Season with salt and pepper. Mix the potato well and keep warm until needed.

Cut the endive in half lengthwise. Heat a large sauté pan over medium heat with 2 tablespoons of butter. Place the endive in the pan with the cut side up. Season the endive with the sugar, salt, and pepper. When the endive has browned on the one side, flip the endive over and continue to cook. After another 2 minutes deglaze the pan with the chicken stock and lemon juice.

Simmer the endive for 8 minutes until cooked through. By this time the chicken stock should have evaporated and the endive will begin to caramelize. Keep the endive warm.

Sauté the last pint of Brussels sprouts with 2 tablespoons of butter in a small sauté pan over medium heat. After 2 minutes of cooking add 1/2 cup of water and let the mixture cook for 3 minutes. By this time the water should have boiled off leaving the cooked Brussels sprouts in a light glaze of butter. Season the sprouts with salt and pepper.

Heat a cast iron or steel sauté pan over a medium high heat. Add some grape seed oil to the pans and place the fish skin side down. Cook the fish for 2 minutes on the stove and transfer to a 400 degree oven without flipping. Cook the fish for 6 minutes in the oven. Remove the fish from the pan and transfer to a warm plate.

Reduce the red wine and the shallots to a paste in a small saucepot over a medium heat. Remove the pot from the heat and whisk in the vinegar and butter. Season with salt and pepper to taste. Keep in a warm place until needed.

To serve, spoon some of the potatoes on each plate. Place the fish next to the potatoes and arrange the endive next to the fish. Spoon equal portions of the Brussels sprouts on each plate. Put one tablespoon of the red wine shallot sauce around the sprouts.

ARCTIC CHAR

with warm potato salad, riesling cabbage, garlic sausage, and grainy mustard sauce

6 fillets of Arctic char *(7 oz. each)*
2 pieces fresh garlic sausage
2 Tbs grape seed oil

POTATOES:

2 lb fingerling potatoes
1 Tbs cumin seeds
1 bay leaf
1 sprig fresh thyme
3 shallots
1 Tbs Dijon mustard
2 Tbs Champagne vinegar
1 cup chicken stock *(see pg. 168)*
⅛ cup grape seed oil
2 Tbs chopped chives

CABBAGE:

16 oz sauerkraut
1 Tbs caraway seeds
1¼ cup dry Riesling wine
1 granny smith apple
1 small Yukon gold potato
6 Tbs butter

PRESENTATION:

3 oz magenta greens
1 Tbs lemon vinaigrette *(see pg. 177)*
½ cup grainy mustard sauce
(see pg. 167)

PREP **40 MINUTES**
COOK **15 MINUTES**
SERVES **6**

Place the whole fingerling potatoes in a pot with enough water to cover them. Put the cumin, baby leaf, thyme and salt in the water. Bring the water to a boil and cook for 2 minutes. Take off the heat, but let the potatoes cool in the cooking water. When the water is room temperature, check the potato for doneness. If they are not done, bring them to a boil again and let them cool in the water one more time. When the potatoes are cooked and cool, remove them and discard the water. Slice the potatoes in 1/8 inch slices. When almost ready to serve dinner, heat the chicken stock to a boil. Mince the shallots with a sharp knife and mix them in a bowl with the mustard, vinegar, and potatoes. Add the hot chicken stock and drizzle in the oil while mixing. Season with salt, pepper and the chopped chives. Leave covered in a warm area until needed.

Drain the sauerkraut. Sauté the cabbage in a pan with 2 tablespoons of the butter and the caraway seeds. Add the wine and reduce by half. Meanwhile, peel and grate the apple and potato separately. Add the apple to the reducing cabbage mixture. When the mixture is almost dry add in the potato. Cook the cabbage until it is nearly dry. Add the remaining butter, 4 tablespoons of fresh Riesling wine, salt and ground white pepper.

If the sausage has already been cooked, simply slice it into 1/8 inch rounds. Warm your cast iron or steel frying pan up over a medium high heat. Sauté the sausage rounds in the pan with 1 tablespoon of the grape seed oil. Remove the sausage and keep them in a warm place. Add more oil if needed and sauté the Artic char fillets on the skin side for 6 minutes. Lower the heat if the skin is getting too dark. Flip the fish and cook for 30 more seconds.

To serve, place a couple of spoons of the potato salad on six individual plates. Divide the cabbage equally between the plates. Put 4 or 5 slices of sausage and the fish on top of the cabbage. Spoon a couple of tablespoons of the sauce on the plates. Mix the magenta greens with the lemon vinaigrette and put it on top of the fish.

SALMON BELLY TARTAR

with pickled daikon, yuzu aioli, and american caviar

2 lbs salmon fillet
2 shallots
1 Tbs sesame oil
2 Tbs ginger juice
2 Tbs grape seed oil

½ lb daikon root
1 cup pickling juice *(see pg. 170)*
6 Tbs yuzu aioli *(see pg. 175)*
1 pint hydroponic mache
6 tsp American sturgeon caviar
6 Tbs soy citrus Juice *(see pg. 181)*

YUZU AIOLI:

1 whole egg
3 Tbs rice wine vinegar
1 Tbs yuzu juice
1 tsp Dijon mustard
¾ cup turmeric oil
(grape seed oil with 1 Tbs tumeric)
¼ cup mustard oil *(from specialty grocer)*

Only use the highest quality salmon from a very trustworthy fishmonger. Dice the salmon into small pieces. Place the salmon in a bowl with the sesame oil and grape seed oil. Grate some fresh ginger until you get the tablespoon of juice needed. Then grate the shallots and add all of the juice and pulp to the bowl. Season the tartar with salt and pepper. Keep refrigerated until needed.

Peel and slice the daikon. Pickle it in the juice for at least 20 minutes.

To make the yuzu aioli, put the egg, yuzu juice, vinegar, and mustard in a blender and purée for 30 seconds. Drizzle in the oil slowly while the blender is on a medium speed. As the sauce begins to thicken, carefully help it to move in the blender with a rubber spatula. Be very careful not to let the blades of the blender hit the spatula. Season the sauce with salt. Store in the refrigerator until needed. Yields 2 cups.

To serve, place some of the daikon on the six plates. Place equal stacks of salmon tartar next to the daikon. Squirt the yuzu aioli around the dish. Place a tablespoon of the soy juice on each tartar stack and follow that with a tablespoon of the caviar. Garnish with a touch of the mache.

PREP **20 MINUTES**
COOK **15 MINUTES**
SERVES **6**

SUBTLE :: SPRINGY :: RICH :: SAVORY

SEAFOOD GLOSSARY

LOBSTER

The popularity of Maine or American Lobster is probably due to the sweet flavor of its meat. It has more tender texture than its southern relative. Lobster always goes well with buttery sauces, and sweet acidity brings out its flavor. I like the tropical spiciness the ginger brings to the dish, and the crunchy vegetables add texture and earthiness.

MONKFISH

A very unattractive cold water fish, the monkfish has a nice mild flavor with very meaty texture. It has always been coined the poor man's lobster due to its chewy character. The smaller monkfish are more tender, especially when they are cooked whole. The risotto gives us a soft buttery texture with the onion and squash for fall earthiness and a chicken-based sauce to add a leaner saltiness.

GROUPER

I like to use the large black grouper because it gives us thicker fillets with more fattiness. This traditional Florida fish has flaky white light flavored meat that hold up well with spiciness. The sticky rice and apricot glaze give the sweetness to the dish. The soy and peanuts give us the saltiness, and the eggplant adds a pepper flavor. The bok choy helps to blend the Asian feel and give a freshness to the dish.

STURGEON

Sturgeon is a pre-historic looking fish with cartilage instead of bones. It is best known for its eggs which we know as caviar. I first worked with the Columbia River sturgeon in San Francisco. It was so fresh that the red of the blood line and the orange fat from the fish make it look painted. It is best cooked through with a good balance of acidity. With the thought of Russian caviar in mind, I balance it with earthy roasted potatoes, and creamy acidic crème fraiche.

SHRIMP

Gulf of Mexico shrimp are one of the truly treasured creatures of our area. Their texture is firm with delicate sweetness lying in their flesh. Smooth avocado helps to balance the crunchy and chewy texture of the tempura shrimp. Acidic Florida citrus and the spicy peppers in the sauce help you to start over with each bite and bring a tropical awareness to the dish.

SWEETWATER PRAWN

The texture of this shrimp gets very mushy when cooked. I would much rather eat this shrimp raw. You can really taste the clean subtle flavors. The pickled cucumber is crunchy and acidic, and the vinaigrette is spicy and nutty in taste. You can also fry the heads of the shrimp until they are very crispy and serve them with some aioli.

MAINE LOBSTER BISQUE
with fennel, leeks, and tarragon

1	large onion
1	fennel bulb
1 bunch	celery
2	large carrots
1	leek
4 Tbs	butter
1 bunch	basil
1 bunch	tarragon
1	bay leaf
1 head	garlic
1 Tbs	black peppercorns
1 cup	cognac
2 cups	dry white wine
1½ cup	basmati rice
2 Tbs	tomato paste
1 gallon	lobster stock *(see pg. 172)*
1 quart	heavy cream

FINISHING GARNISH:

1	fennel bulb
1	leek
1	onion
2 Tbs	butter
1 bunch	tarragon
1 cup	whipped cream
3	lobsters
1 gallon	court bouillon

Chop the onions, fennel, celery, and carrots and sauté them in 4 tablespoons of butter in a large soup pot. Let the vegetables cook for 5 minutes and add the tomato paste. Cook for an additional 2 minutes before deglazing with the cognac. Cook the cognac until the mixture is dry, and then add the white wine. Cook down again until the white wine is gone. Add the basil, tarragon, bay leaf, halved garlic, peppercorns, and lobster stock. Bring the soup to a boil and turn down to simmer for 10 minutes. Add the rice and cook for 15 more minutes. Add the cream and let the soup return to a boil. Remove the bisque from the heat and let it cool for 15 minutes at room temperature. Carefully blend the soup in small batches in a blender. Pass the bisque through a fine strainer. Season the bisque with salt, pepper, and more cognac or cream if needed.

Bring the court bouillon to a boil. Place the lobsters in the broth and simmer them for 4 minutes. Take the broth off the heat and let the lobsters cool in the liquid. Remove the lobsters from the broth and clean the meat from the claws and tail. Cut each tail in half. Dice the fennel, white part of the leek, and the onion. Sauté them in 2 tablespoons of butter for 3 minutes. Season them with salt and pepper.

To serve, place the half of the lobster in each bowl. Place a tablespoon of whipped cream next to the lobster. Spoon a couple of tablespoons of the vegetable mixture in the bowl. Put a few sprigs of tarragon on each lobster, and pour the hot soup over all the ingredients.

PREP **20 MINUTES**
COOK **50 MINUTES**
SERVES **6**

MAINE LOBSTER

with spinach, snap peas, pearl onions, red pepper, and tokaji ginger sauce

6 **Maine lobsters** *(1½lb each)*
4 Tbs **butter**
1 lb **baby spinach**
1 pint **pearl onions**
1 **red pepper**
1 large **handful snap peas**
2 gal **court bouillon** *(see pg. 168)*
1 cup **Tokaji ginger sauce**

TOKAJI GINGER SAUCE:

1 **3-inch piece fresh ginger root**
(peeled and julienne)
1 cup **Tokaji wine**
1 Tbs **vanilla extract**
(½ vanilla bean is better if available)
¼ lb **butter** *(cubed and cold)*
1 Tbs **chopped cilantro**

Bring the court bouillon to a boil. Place the lobsters in the broth and simmer them for 2 minutes. Take the broth off the heat and let the lobsters cool in the liquid. Remove the lobsters from the broth and clean the meat from the claws and tail. Reserve the tail to use in the presentation. Freeze the head and shells for lobster bisque. Keep the lobster chilled until needed.

To heat before serving, put the lobster meat with 1 cup of the cooking liquid and 4 tablespoons of butter in a pan and warm in the oven at 350 degrees for 2 minutes or until warm, but do not boil.

Peel the pepper and slice the flesh into thin strips. Clean the snap pea of the stem and blanch in boiling water for 1 minute. Blanch the pearl onions in boiling water for 5 minutes. Shock both of the vegetables in ice water to stop cooking. Cut off the root end, and squeeze off the outer skin of the pearl onion. In a sauté pan, melt 2 tablespoons of butter and cook the pearl onions, snap peas and pepper strips for 3 minutes. Season with salt and pepper. Transfer to a warm plate. Place 2 more tablespoons of butter in the same pan and cook the spinach for 1 minute. Season the spinach with salt and pepper.

In a small saucepot over a medium high heat, reduce the ginger, wine, and vanilla to a paste. Remove from the heat and whisk in the butter on piece at a time. Season with the lime juice, cilantro, salt, and pepper.

To serve, place equal portions of the spinach on six plates. Position the shell on the bed of spinach. Spoon the vegetables in the shell with the lobster and drizzle the lobster meat with a tablespoon of the ginger sauce.

PREP **30 MINUTES**
COOK **15 MINUTES**
SERVES **6**

FLORIDA SPINY LOBSTER
with green curry coconut sauce

6 spiny lobsters *(1 lb each)*
1 gal court bouillon *(see pg. 168)*
1 onion
2 shallots
1 Tbs ginger
6 cloves garlic
2 Tbs lemongrass
2 Tbs peanut oil
1 Tbs green curry paste
1 Tbs cane sugar *(liquid)*
1 tsp coriander seeds *(crushed)*
1 cup chicken stock *(see pg. 168)*
2 cups water
1 bunch cilantro
2 limes
3 cans coconut milk

2 cups Jasmine rice
3 cups water

Bring the court bouillon to a boil and add in the lobsters. Boil the mixture for 3 minutes. Remove the pot from the heat and let the lobsters cool in the water. Remove the lobsters and twist off their tail. Discard the head of the lobster or keep it if you want to garnish with it. The spiny lobster head does not make a great stock. Cut the tail of the lobster in half lengthwise. Loosen the meat in the shell, but do not remove it completely.

To make the sauce, chop the onion, shallots, ginger, and lemongrass. Smash the garlic cloves. Heat a small sauce pot over medium high heat. Add the oil and sauté the onion, shallots, ginger, lemongrass, and garlic for 3 minutes. Add the green curry paste and cane sugar and cook for 2 more minutes. Pour in the chicken stock, water, and coriander and bring the mixture to a boil. Simmer until the liquid has reduced by half. Add the coconut milk and let the sauce come to a boil and reduce the liquid by half. Remove the sauce from heat and add in the cilantro. Purée the mixture in a bar blender and strain. Season the sauce with salt and the lime juice.

Bring the rice, water, and salt to a boil. Turn the heat down and cook the rice covered for 12 minutes. Turn off the heat and let the rice continue to steam for 5 more minutes.

Place the lobster shells in a sauté pan and pour the curry sauce over them. Bring the sauce to a boil and baste the lobsters with it for a couple of minutes. When the lobsters have cooked through, place them on a plate with the rice and spoon the curry sauce around.

PREP 30 MINUTES
COOK 15 MINUTES
SERVES 6

WHOLE ROASTED BABY MONKFISH

with butternut squash risotto, cipollini onions, and rosemary veal jus

6	baby monkfish *(1 lb each, head off)*
6 Tbs	grape seed oil
9 Tbs	butter
5 oz	Arborio rice
1½ Tbs	olive oil
1 small	shallots
1 large	butternut squash
½ cup	dry white wine
2 cups	chicken stock
½ cup	water
1	lime
15	Italian cipollini onions
2 cups	veal stock *(see pg. 169)*
1 sprig	rosemary

PREP **60 MINUTES**
COOK **15 MINUTES**
SERVES **6**

Peel the squash and cut perfect little squares from the flesh. Any imperfect scraps should be boiled in enough salted water to cover them. When the scraps are soft, drain them of the water and purée them in a bar blender. Save this for later as well as the perfect pieces. The rice will take the longest to cook so we will start that first. Warm the olive oil in a heavy bottomed stock pot over medium high heat and add in the nicely minced shallots. When the shallots have cooked 2 minutes, add the rice and stir it with a wooden spoon to coat all of the grains with oil. Deglaze the rice with the white wine. Cook the rice until all the wine is gone. Add chicken stock 1/2 cup at a time, constantly stirring to help develop the starchy creaminess of the rice, cook for 22 minutes. On the last cup of stock, add in the perfect raw diced squash. When the rice has only a slight bite left to it, add in the purée and the last 2 tablespoons of butter. Season the risotto with salt and pepper and a squeeze of the lime juice. The risotto cannot wait too long before serving.

Meanwhile, wash the cipollini onions in water and remove any dirt. Toss them with a table-spoon of olive oil, salt and pepper. Roast them for 10 minutes in a 400 degree oven. Remove them and peel off the outer skin and discard. Keep them warm until serving.

Ask your fishmonger for the smallest monkfish he can find. Have him remove the head, skin, and trim the fish so it is only showing the snowy white flesh. Leave the fish on the bone.

Heat a cast iron or steel fish skillet over a medium high flame Add 1 tablespoon of grape seed oil to the pan and give it 20 seconds to get hot. Season the fish with salt and fresh ground pepper. Place the fish gently in the oil and sauté it on the stove for 1 minute. Place one table-spoon of the butter in the pan and transfer the skillet to the 400 degree oven. Roast the fish for about 10 minutes. The meat of the fish should be firm and pulling away from the center bone. Repeat the process for the other 5 fish. Place the fish on a warm plate with the oven off and let them remain warm.

Reduce the veal stock by two thirds in a small sauce pan. Whisk in 1 tablespoon of butter and infuse the rosemary sprig in the sauce to pick up some fresh rosemary flavor.

To serve, spoon the soft creamy risotto on a large plate and place the whole fish around it. Place a few of the roasted onions on each plate and spoon a generous amount of the sauce around.

GLAZED BLACK GROUPER

with thai sweet rice, baby eggplant, bok choy, and coconut curry sauce

3 lbs	black grouper fillet
2 Tbs	sesame oil
2 Tbs	brown sugar
4 each	green onions
4 oz	soy sauce
2 cups	sticky Thai sweet white rice
1 cup	water
1 can	coconut milk
1 Tbs	salt
1 head	baby bok choy
1 Tbs	soy sauce
1 tsp	sesame oil
1 Tbs	butter
20	baby eggplant
2 cups	olive oil
2 Tbs	honey
4 Tbs	balsamic vinegar
1	sprig thyme
2	shallots
2 Tbs	coriander seed
1	bay leaf
1 cup	coconut curry sauce *(see pg. 175)*
½ cup	sweet soy glaze *(see pg. 181)*

PREP **40 MINUTES**
COOK **15 MINUTES**
SERVES **6**

Cut the grouper fillet into perfect 7-ounce pieces. Chop the scraps and sauté them with sesame oil in a non-stick pan over medium heat. Cook for 30 seconds until cooked only halfway. Transfer the grouper while hot to a bowl with the brown sugar, chopped green onions, and soy sauce, then stir it well. Let the mixture cool. Keep it in the refrigerator until you are ready to wrap the sticky rice rolls.

Score the bottom of the baby eggplant leaving them whole, but flesh exposed. Mince the shallots and warm them in a couple of tablespoons of the oil in a small pot. Add the honey and cook for 20 seconds. Deglaze with the vinegar and cook 30 more seconds. Add the thyme, eggplant, and the rest of the oil. Season the oil with salt, coriander, bay leaf, and pepper. Cook the eggplant over a very low flame for 15 minutes, or until tender. Keep in the oil until needed.

To cook the rice, place the rice, water, coconut milk, and salt in a small sauce pot and warm over medium high heat until simmering. Stir the rice every 30 seconds for 2 minutes. Lower the heat and cover the rice for the next 15 minutes. Stir the rice 4-5 times during that period. Remove the rice from the heat and let it sit covered for 10 more minutes. Lay the rice out on a sheet pan to cool at room temperature.

Lay a sheet of plastic wrap out and spoon 3 ounces of rice on to it. Flatten the rice and place a tablespoon of the grouper mixture in the middle of the rice. Pick up the edges of the plastic and fold the rice over to create a package. Twist the plastic to seal the package from any air or liquid. Keep in the refrigerator until needed. You can make these a day in advance. To heat the package before serving, you can steam or boil the rice in the plastic for 5 minutes.

Clean the grill and heat it as hot as possible. Season the grouper with salt, pepper and oil. Place the fillets on the grill for 3 minutes on each side. Glaze the fish with the sweet soy glaze and move them to the top warming rack of the grill. Let them roast there for 2 more minutes with the lid down.

In a small non-stick pan, warm the butter and the sesame oil. Add the bok choy and cook for 30 seconds. Pour in the soy sauce and sauté for 1 more minute.

Remove the plastic from the rice packages and place them on the six plates. Set 3 warm eggplants on each plate. Divide the bok choy between the plates. Place a piece of fish on each plate. Spoon the chili sauce around.

fig **124**

COLUMBIA RIVER STURGEON

with butterball potatoes, crème fraiche, caviar, and vodka beet vinaigrette

6	fillets of American sturgeon
	(7 oz. each)
4 Tbs	olive oil
2 lbs	baby roasting potatoes *(C size)*
2	bay leaves
1 sprig	thyme
1 cup	crème fraiche *(sub sour cream)*
1	lemon
2	shallots
1 cup	vodka beet vinaigrette *(see pg. 178)*
2 oz	American sturgeon caviar
1 pkg	parsley micro greens

Place the potatoes in a small pot and cover them with cold water. Season the water with a strong pinch of salt, the bay leaves, and thyme sprig. Bring the water to a boil and remove it from the heat. Let the potatoes cool in the liquid. If you are using a larger potato you might have to bring the water to a boil one more time. When the potatoes have completely cooled in the water, remove them and keep refrigerated until needed. Discard the water.

Mix the crème fraiche with the juice of the lemon and the shallots which you will need to mince nicely. Season the cream with salt and fresh ground white pepper. Keep refrigerated until needed.

Heat a steel or cast iron fish skillet over a medium high flame. Season the sturgeon with sea salt and freshly cracked black pepper. Add 2 tablespoons of the olive oil to the hot pan and carefully place the fish in the pan. Do not overcrowd your frying pan. If there is not an inch of space on each side of the fish, you might have to cook it in two pans. Cook the fish for one minute on the stove top. Place the cooked potatoes around the skillet with the fish and without turning the fish place the whole skillet in a 400 degree oven for 8 minutes. Remove the fish from the pan and serve it with the golden brown side facing up. Sturgeon is a fish I like to cook completely thorough.

To serve, place a piece of fish on each plate. Spoon some of your crème fraiche on the plate and arrange the potatoes on top. Spoon an equal portion of caviar over the potatoes. Drizzle the vodka beet vinaigrette over the fish and the plate. Sprinkle some of the parsley sprouts around.

PREP **30 MINUTES**
COOK **10 MINUTES**
SERVES **6**

SESAME GULF SHRIMP

with avocado purée and florida citrus sauce

18	gulf shrimp *(U-10 size)*
1 cup	flour
1 cup	soda water
pinch	sesame seeds
pinch	baking soda
6 cups	peanut oil
3	avocados
2 Tbs	sesame oil
2	limes
1	shallot
1 cup	Florida citrus sauce *(see pg. 180)*

Whisk the flour, sesame seeds, baking soda, soda water and salt. Chill the batter in the refrigerator until needed. Clean the shells from the body of the shrimp and de-vein them. Heat the oil in a small deep fryer to 350 degrees. Dip the shrimp in the batter while holding the tail fins. Carefully, dip the shrimp three quarters of the way into the oil and hold it there for 4 seconds before letting it go. Repeat the process for all the shrimp. You will have to fry the shrimp in batches of 3-4 at a time. Transfer them to a warm plate covered with a paper towel. Season them with fine sea salt when they come out of the oil.

Purée the flesh of the avocado with the sesame oil, lime juice, minced shallot, and salt.

Spoon equal amounts of the avocado purée on each of the six plates. Position 3 of the shrimp in the avocado purée. Drizzle 2 tablespoons of the citrus sauce around.

PREP 30 MINUTES
COOK 10 MINUTES
SERVES 6

SASHIMI OF SWEETWATER PRAWNS

with pickled cucumber and soy vinaigrette

6 whole fresh water prawns
2 Japanese cucumbers
2 cups pickling juice *(see pg. 170)*
12 Tbs soy vinaigrette *(see pg. 179)*

Peel the prawns and clean the shell from the tail meat. Slice the tail down the center being careful not to cut completely through. Rinse the tail meat with cold water to remove any grit. Season the shrimp with fine sea salt and marinate in the soy vinaigrette. Keep very cold until needed.

Slice the cucumbers in long thin strips. Place the cucumbers in the pickling juice for 1 hour. Remove the cucumber from the pickling juice and season with sea salt.

PREP **10 MINUTES**
COOK **3 MINUTES**
SERVES **6**

To serve, place equal amounts of the cucumber slice on small serving plates. Place one of the prawns on each plate. Spoon the soy vinaigrette over the prawns and serve while very cold.

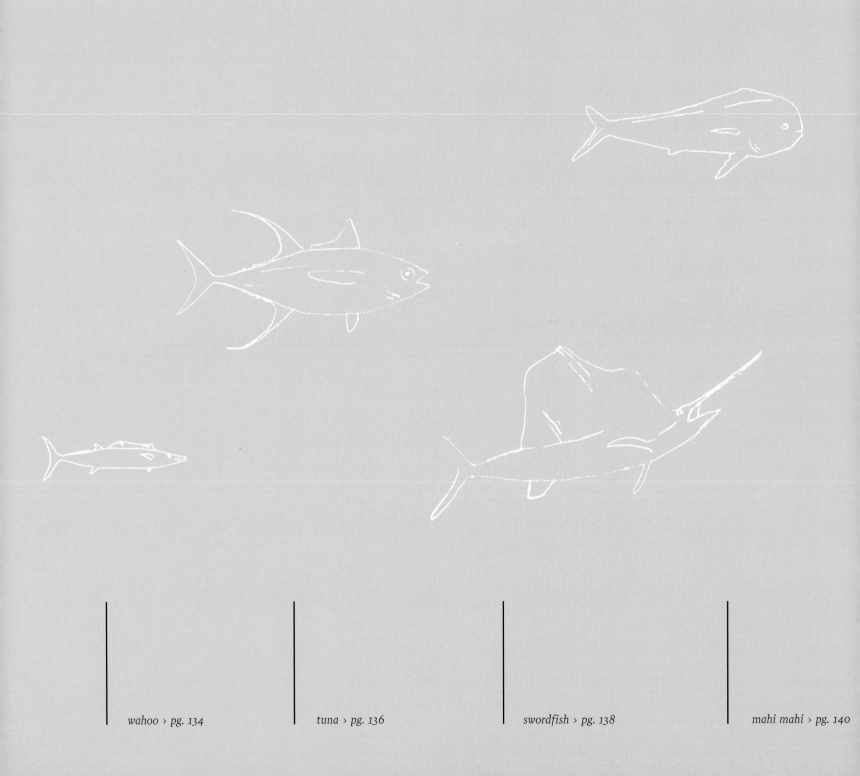

BOLD :: ROBUST :: MEATY :: FIRM

SEAFOOD GLOSSARY

DOLPHIN FISH

Popular by its Hawaiian name, mahi mahi, the dolphin fish, not the mammal, is a very popular sport and eating fish for Floridians. It has firm white meat and sweet flavor. Growing up grilling dolphin on the weekends makes me feel like it's the only way it should be eaten. I like it simple with acidic summer tomatoes and dill, and the egg gribiche which gives the dish some moist flavor dimension.

OPAH

The opah is a giant Pacific moonfish probably close in relation with the permit. It has lean sweet meat that can get tough when cooked fully through. I like to serve it similar to tuna. The cool cucumber and mint go well with the fresh taste of the rare fish. The earthy spice of the callaloo add texture and flavor. The sweet and sour of the tomato add acidity to the dish.

WAHOO

Wahoo is the king daddy of the mackerel family. It has similar characteristics of its close relative, the tuna. Hawaiians call it, Ono, for sweet. It is indeed sweet, and to me best under-cooked. Here, I serve it raw with spicy jalapeño and chive. The pickled freshness of the carrot add a crunchy texture to the dish. I love the smooth texture of aioli with tartar. The flavor of the carrot reminds me of the pickled vegetables you get with your meals in Mexico. The mint and cumin flavor keeps us in that theme.

TUNA

The good thing about the sushi craze of the nineties is that now people will actually eat their tuna medium rare with no problem. Tuna is like salmon in the way that it is an oily fish, but gets very dry when fully cooked. Both fish lose their subtle flavors when cooked too much, and a more powerful fishy taste prevails. The texture of the tuna is balanced in this dish with the creaminess of the chickpea purée. Using chick peas reminds me of the Mediterranean, so I use flavors from that area to accent.

SWORDFISH

Swordfish is a flavorful firm fish that can become dry when overcooked. Its meat is oily and dense and needs acidity and soft textures to balance its strength. The crunchy texture of the bread and bitter arugula are a great balance. The salty pine nuts and sweet currants work well with the acidic balsamic and earthy basil oil. Nothing is too strong to overpower the interesting flavor of this fish.

JOHN DORY

The John Dory is a regal silver fish with a firm texture and fine flake. It is like a pompano without the oiliness. I like to balance this mild fish with the acidity of the tomato broth. The gnocchi make a good contrast in texture, and the aioli add a bit of creaminess. You could substitute a small flat fish if you have trouble finding this variety.

WAHOO TARTAR

with spicy pickled carrots, micro greens, and cumin mint aioli

1 lb	sushi-quality wahoo
4	sweet summer carrots
1	serrano pepper
2 cups	pickling juice *(see pg. 170)*
1 Tbs	olive oil
1 Tbs	chopped chives
6 Tbs	cumin mint aioli *(see pg. 174)*
3 oz	tiny herb greens
1 tsp	lemon vinaigrette *(see pg. 177)*

Peel and cut the carrots in perfect, long strips. Place them in a bowl and cover the carrots with the spicy pickling juice. Let the carrots marinate for at least 1 hour.

Wahoo is a great meaty and mild fish we get fresh all the time in Florida. You can easily substitute any mild fish you get in your area of the world. You need to buy a super fresh fillet from only the fish vendors you trust.

Slice the fish in long thin strips. Lay the strips down and slice them into long, thin julienne pieces. Turn the strips sideways to cut tiny cubes. Place the fish in a bowl and keep cold in the refrigerator.

Slice the flesh from the serrano pepper and discard the seeds and stem. Mince the flesh into tiny pieces and add it to the fish. Mix the fish with the chopped chives, olive oil, salt and pepper. Mix the tiny herb greens with the lemon vinaigrette.

To serve, mold equal amounts of the tartar on to six plates. Place a pile of the pickled carrots on each plate and cover with a small pinch of the herb greens. Drizzle a tablespoon of cumin mint aioli on each plate.

PREP **60 MINUTES**
COOK **2 MINUTES**
SERVES **6**

GULF OF MEXICO RARE TUNA SALAD
with fennel, capers, and olive vinaigrette

2 lbs sushi grade ahi tuna

CHICKPEA PURÉE:

12 oz dried chickpeas
(soak refrigerated overnight in water)

3 qts water

6 cloves garlic

1 bay leaf

1 small onion

1 celery rib

1 lemon

1 cup extra virgin olive oil

black olive vinaigrette *(see pg. 177)*

3 Tbs tiny capers

1 bulb fennel

4 Tbs olive oil

Get a perfect center cut piece of no. 1 sushi grade tuna, cut in one long log from your fish-monger. Season the tuna with salt and cracked pepper. Heat a sauté pan with 1 tablespoon of olive oil and sear the tuna on all sides for 15 seconds per side. Remove the tuna and transfer to a plate to let cool. Spoon the black olive vinaigrette on the tuna and place the tuna in the refrigerator until needed.

Place the chickpeas in a pot of cold water. Wrap the bay leaf, chopped small onion, fennel scraps, celery rib, and 4 of the cloves of garlic (smashed) in a sachet bag, or cheese cloth. You can simply put the ingredients in the water without the bag, but you will need to fish them out later. Bring the chickpeas to a boil and turn down the flame to a very light simmer. Cook the peas until they are soft. Remove the chickpeas and purée in a blender with the 2 raw garlic cloves, lemon juice and olive oil. Season with salt and pepper. Keep chilled until needed.

Trim the root and tops from the fennel bulb and use them in the chickpea sachet. Slice the fennel bulb into 6 1/2-inch slices. Drizzle the fennel with some olive oil and salt and pepper and roast in a 350-degree oven for 10 minutes on a cookie sheet.

To serve, slice six equal portions of the tuna and spoon the vinaigrette around the plate. Serve a mound of the chickpea purée on the tuna and lay the cooled fennel against it. Brush the tuna with olive oil and sprinkle with capers.

PREP **20 MINUTES**
COOK **10 MINUTES**
SERVES **6**

ROASTED SWORDFISH

with olive oil bread, pine nuts, currants, and aged balsamic

6	swordfish steaks *(7 oz. each)*
1	lemon
1 lb	baby arugula
6 Tbs	pine nuts
6 Tbs	dried black currants
6 Tbs	25-year-old balsamic vinegar
12 Tbs	extra virgin olive oil
2 Tbs	butter
6	thick slices of ciabatta bread
6 Tbs	basil oil

BASIL OIL:

2 bunch	basil *(pick leaves only)*
1 cup	extra virgin olive oil

Season the swordfish with salt and cracked pepper. Heat a cast iron or steel fish skillet over a medium high heat. Put 2 tablespoons of olive oil in the hot skillet. Place the swordfish fillets in the skillet and sauté 5 minutes on both sides. Remove the fish from the pan and transfer to a warm plate until needed. Drizzle with lemon juice.

Cut the crust from the ciabatta bread to make 6 equal planks. Season the bread with a tablespoon of olive oil, salt, and pepper. Grill the bread on an open fire or toast the bread in the oven if you do not have a grill readily available. You can grill the swordfish rather than pan roast as well.

In a sauté pan, warm the butter and 3 tablespoons of olive oil until hot. Add the pine nuts and black currants and continue to warm. Quickly add the arugula and toss to coat with the mixture. Drizzle 3 tablespoons of the balsamic over the salad. Season with salt and pepper.

For the basil oil, blanch the basil by plunging it in boiling water for 20 seconds and then shocking it in ice water. Squeeze the water from the basil and purée it in a blender with the olive oil until smooth. Season the purée with salt and white pepper. Warm one cup of basil purée until it begins to bubble and is close to a boil. Remove the purée from the heat and strain it through a fine sieve. Let the mixture cool in a glass container until it has separated. Skim the green basil oil from the top and discard the juice on the bottom.

To serve, place a piece of bread in the center of each plate. Spoon equal portions of the arugula mixture over the bread. Place the warm fish on top of the salad. Spoon any juice from the pan back over the fish. Drizzle the balsamic and basil oil around the plate.

PREP 20 MINUTES
COOK 10 MINUTES
SERVES 6

fig **139**

GRILLED MAHI MAHI
with dill roasted tomatoes and sauce gribiche

6 mahi mahi fillets *(7 oz. each)*
2 Tbs olive oil
2 lemons
9 large vine ripe tomatoes
1 Tbs chopped garlic
2 shallots
1 bunch dill
1 cup extra virgin olive oil
12 Tbs sauce gribiche

SAUCE GRIBICHE:

3 hard boiled eggs *(diced)*
1 large red onion *(diced)*
2 Tbs capers
¼ cup black olives *(pitted)*
2 anchovies *(minced)*
1 Tbs Dijon mustard
1 lemon *(juiced)*
2 Tbs Champagne vinegar
2 Tbs chopped parsley
¼ cup extra virgin olive oil

Wash and cut the core out of the tomatoes. Slice the tomatoes in half from top to bottom. Squeeze out the seeds and place the tomatoes in a bowl. Mince the shallots and add them to the tomatoes with the garlic. Clean the stems from the dill and chop the leaves roughly. Toss the dill and the olive oil with the tomato mixture. Season the tomatoes with salt and pepper. Lay the tomatoes flat side down in a baking dish. Pour the oil, shallots, garlic, and dill on top of the tomatoes. Roast the mixture in the oven at 350 degrees for 20 minutes. Remove the tomatoes from the oven and let them cool. Remove the skins from the tomatoes.

Heat a grill on the highest setting. Brush the grill clean before cooking. Season the fish with salt, pepper, and the olive oil. Place the fish on the grill and cook for 4 minutes. Flip the fish and cook for an additional 4 minutes. Transfer to a warm plate and season with the lemon juice.

For the sauce gribiche, mix in a bowl the anchovies, mustard, lemon, and olive oil until combined. Fold in the eggs, red onion, capers, olives and parsley. Season with salt and pepper.

To serve, place 3 tomato halves on each of the six plates. Lay the grilled fish on top of the tomatoes. Drizzle the tomato pan juice around the fish. Serve two spoonfuls of the gribiche on the side of the fish.

PREP **45 MINUTES**
COOK **15 MINUTES**
SERVES **6**

HAWAIIAN OPAH
with wilted callaloo, tomato chutney, and cumin mint aioli

4 lb	opah fish, center cut loin
2 Tbs	garam marsala
4 Tbs	olive oil
1 lb	callaloo
1	lime
4 Tbs	unsalted butter
1 cup	tomato chutney
1 cup	cumin mint aioli *(see pg. 174)*

TOMATO CHUTNEY:

2 cups	tomato flesh
	(diced, no seeds or skin)
2	shallots *(minced)*
1 Tbs	grape seed oil
¼ cup	sugar
¼ cup	Champagne vinegar
1 Tbs	garam marsala

Have the fishmonger cut you two, 2-pound pieces of fish. Make sure they are only 2 inches in width.

Season the fish with the garam marsala, salt and black pepper. Heat a heavy cast iron or steel sauté pan over a medium high flame. Place the fish in the pan and sauté it for 1 minute on each side. Place the fish in a warm area until ready to serve.

Clean the callaloo of the thick stems and chop the leaves into smaller pieces. Wash the leaves to remove any dirt and pat them dry. Melt the butter in a sauté pan over medium high heat. Add the callaloo to the pan and cook for 3 minutes. Season with salt and pepper. Squeeze the lime juice over the callaloo before serving.

For the tomato chutney, warm the shallots with the oil for a couple of minutes in a small pot over a medium heat. Add in the sugar and garam marsala and let them melt together. Deglaze with the vinegar and add in the tomato. Reduce the mixture gently for just under an hour allowing the liquid to cook down. Season with salt and pepper.

In a small saucepot, bring the cumin mint sauce to a boil. Whisk it vigorously before serving.

To serve, cut thin slices of the opah with a very sharp knife. Place the warm callaloo on the plate and arrange the opah slices around it. Equally distribute the chutney between the six plates. Whisk the sauce again and spoon the light frothy milk around the plate.

PREP **30 MINUTES**
COOK **10 MINUTES**
SERVES **6**

GRILLED JOHN DORY

with ratatouille vegetables, potato gnocchi, tomato broth, and basil aioli

6 John Dory fillets (*7 oz. each*)
11 Tbs olive oil
1 red bell pepper
1 yellow bell pepper
1 yellow squash
1 zucchini
1 purple eggplant
1 Tbs garlic confit
1 sprig thyme
2 lemons
6 Tbs basil aioli (*see pg. 174*)
6 oz tomato broth

POTATO GNOCCHI:

3 lbs Idaho potatoes
1 Tbs butter
5 oz semolina
1 Tbs flour
5 egg yolks

TOMATO BROTH:

3 cups fresh tomato juice
2 shallots (*minced*)
2 Tbs garlic confit (*see pg. 172*)
2 sprigs parsley, thyme, and basil (*each*)
pinch sugar
¼ cup extra virgin olive oil

PREP 60 MINUTES
COOK 40 MINUTES
SERVES 6

For the gnocchi: bake the potatoes in the oven at 350 degrees. When the potatoes are tender, peel them and push them through a potato ricer. Let the potato cool to a warm feel. Weigh out 31 ounces of milled potato and add the semolina, flour, and egg yolks. You can either roll the dough out with flour by hand into long cigar shapes and cut small circles, or you can place the dough in a piping bag with a round straight tip, and cut the shapes right from the piping bag into salted boiling water. When the gnocchi float to the top scoop them out and shock them in ice cold water. Drain them and toss them in olive oil to keep them from sticking together. Heat 1 tablespoon of butter in a non-stick pan over medium high heat. Add the gnocchi and sauté them until they have browned on both sides.

For the tomato broth, simmer the tomato, shallots, garlic, herbs, and sugar, over a medium heat until the liquid is reduced by two thirds. Season the broth with salt and pepper. Strain the broth and purée in a blender with the olive oil. Reseason with salt to taste.

To make the vegetables, cut each item into small equal sized portions. In a sauté pan over medium high heat, cook each item separately in a tablespoon of the olive oil, salt and pepper for 3 minutes. Combine all the ingredients back together in the pan with the garlic confit and thyme leaves. Keep the vegetables warm while you cook the fish.

Rub the John Dory fillets with olive oil and season with salt and pepper. Get the grill very hot and clean it well with an oiled rag. Place the fish on the hot grill and let it cook for 4 minutes. Flip over the fish and cook for an additional 2 minutes. Remove the fish from the grill and place it on a plate in a warm area. Squeeze some drops of the fresh lemon juice over the fillet.

To serve, place equal amounts of the vegetables on six plates. Divide the gnocchi and spoon them around the outside of the plate. Lay the fish over the vegetables and spoon the warm tomato broth around the plate. Put a dollop of aioli on the side of the plate.

STRONG :: UNIQUE :: EARTHY :: TEXTURAL

SEAFOOD GLOSSARY

SNAIL

I have always enjoyed the chewy excitement of snails. Maybe, it's the fond memories of my first restaurant job as a teenager. It was a small French restaurant which had a popular snail dish that I loved. We get our snails from the Pacific Northwest where they raise a small version of the French cousin. They feed the snails basil to purge them of any sand or grit in their system. I like to pair them with the nutty flavor of the sun choke. The truffle oil in the purée gives the dish an earthy feel and the prosciutto adds the salt. The soft texture of the ravioli balances the mild chewiness of the snails. The acidity of the red wine sauce awakens the taste buds to the subtle flavors of all these delightful ingredients.

CONCH

Conch is a tropical edible marine snail. I probably love conch seviche due to the great memories of it as a kid. We used to go to the Bahamas for the summer, and the locals would pluck the conch straight from the water, marinate and mix it with a salad on the beach before your eyes. I could eat it all day long. In this recipe, I use more tender farm-raised queen conch and give it a spicy sweet twist. The sweet of the carrot and conch gang up on the super spicy of the habanera with the lime juice acting as the referee in this wrestling match of flavors. The fresh vegetables add crunchy texture and a neutral balance for the other flavors.

CALAMARI

These fresh baby squid are delicate in flavor and are more melting in texture than their larger family members. They pair well with the grainy corn flavor of the polenta. The lemon and parsley do not overpower the subtle flavors of this dish, but add the acidity needed to bring out its simplicity.

OCTOPUS

On my first visit to Greece, I discovered the mild chewiness of the octopus. It's lightness pairs so well with the acidity of the lemon juice and pepperiness of the virgin olive oil. The salty flavor of the olive reminds me of the Mediterranean where this eight-armed creature is surely adorned.

CLAM

Anyone who has gone clam digging as a kid can bring back childhood memories with the salty chewiness of these wonderful creatures. Clams are hearty little guys that can hold up to strong pairings of spice and acidity. I like pairing ham, sausage, or bacon with clams. The smoky bacon and peppery piquillo are a great match in this dish.

RAZOR CLAM

Razor clams are an interesting version to the more prevalent little neck and manila varieties. Like a steamer clam, the razor clam's downfall is its tendency to be overly gritty. You can rinse the clams in water really well, and soak them in heavily salted water to get rid of as much sand as possible before cooking. I like to blanch them first and clean the clam of its grit, and then re-cook it with a flavorful, and spicy sauce. The clam has great chewy texture that does well with flavor-forward pairings.

BASIL SNAILS

with sun choke ravioli, prosciutto, and barolo wine sauce

1 lb fresh basil snails

3 shallots

¼ lb prosciutto

1 lemon

8 Tbs unsalted butter

2 Tbs grated Parmesan cheese

18 sun choke ravioli *(see pg. 183)*

1 cup Barolo wine sauce

BAROLO WINE SAUCE:

2 cups Barolo wine

3 Tbs balsamic vinegar

4 shallots

1 Tbs cream

¼ lb butter *(cubed and cold)*

PREP **60 MINUTES**
COOK **20 MINUTES**
SERVES **6**

Bring a pot of salted water to a boil. Toss in the ravioli and cook them at a gentle boil for 3 minutes. Meanwhile, warm the butter up in a large sauté pan over medium heat. Let the butter start to brown and pull it off the heat. When the ravioli is done, strain and transfer them to the brown butter. Sprinkle them with the cheese and baste them with the brown butter. Season them with salt and pepper.

Ask your butcher if he has the heel of the prosciutto which is the end where it gets too small to make nice slices. You should get this at a lower price, yet it still has great flavor. We get natural Oregon snails which have been fed basil to purge their system. You can substitute the French canned variety if you have no source for the snails. Heat the butter up in a sauté pan over a medium high heat. Dice the prosciutto as well as the shallots. Add the shallots and prosciutto and let them sauté for 2 minutes. Rinse the snails in cold water and drain them. Place them in the sauté pan with the shallots and ham. Sauté the snails for 2 more minutes. Season the snails with salt, pepper, and the lemon juice.

To make the wine sauce, reduce the wine, vinegar, and shallots over a medium heat in a small saucepot until almost completely dry. Add in the cream and whisk in the butter one piece at a time. Season with salt and pepper. Strain the sauce and keep warm until needed.

To serve, place equal amounts of ravioli on each plate. Spoon the snail mixture over the ravioli and drizzle a couple of tablespoons of Barolo wine sauce around the plate.

FARM-RAISED QUEEN CONCH
with carrot habanera juice

2 cups baby queen conch meat
1 green bell pepper *(diced)*
1 carrots *(peeled and diced)*
1 red bell pepper *(diced)*
2 ribs celery *(diced)*
1 red onion *(diced)*
1 cucumber *(peeled, seeded, and diced)*
2 limes
1 bunch cilantro

CARROT HABANERA JUICE:
2 shallots
1 habanera pepper
2 cloves garlic
1 Tbs olive oil
1 tsp ground nutmeg
1 tsp cumin seeds
4 each whole cloves
2 cups carrot juice
2 limes

Baby queen conch is much smaller than the large conch that gives us those beautiful shells. The queen conch does not need to be tenderized. Simply cut the conch into smaller pieces and mix the conch with chopped vegetables and let them marinate for 1 hour.

To make the carrot habanera juice, chop the shallots, habanera pepper, and garlic. Sauté them in a small sauce pan with the olive oil. When they have cooked for 1 minute, add the nutmeg, cumin seeds, and cloves and cook for 30 more seconds. Add the carrot juice and bring the mixture to a boil. Reduce the juice by half. Strain the juice and let it cool to room temperature. Season the juice with salt and the lime juice. Refrigerate until needed.

When you are ready to serve, place the conch in 6 martini glasses or serving bowls. Pour the chilled infused carrot juice over the conch salad.

PREP **15 MINUTES**
COOK **5 MINUTES**
SERVES **6**

BABY CALAMARI
with polenta and lemon parsley sauce

12 baby squid
4 oz polenta
6 cups chicken stock *(see pg. 168)*
½ cup extra virgin olive oil
3 lemons *(juiced)*

1 cup white wine
1 cup fish stock *(see pg. 169)*
8 Tbs butter
1 Tbs garlic confit *(see pg. 172)*
1 bunch Italian flat leaf parsley
(finely chopped)

Bring the chicken stock to a boil in a large sauce pot. Whisk in the polenta and turn the heat down to a simmer. Stir the polenta frequently over the next 40 minutes. Whisk in the olive oil. Season with salt, pepper, and the juice of one lemon. Let the polenta cool until it has slightly thickened. Spoon the bodies of the squid with the polenta and reserve any left over polenta for later.

Place the calamari in a oven proof sauté pan with the 2 tablespoons of the butter, wine, fish stock, garlic, and the juice of 1 lemon. Bake the seafood in a 350 degree oven for 10 minutes. Remove the calamari from the pan and place 2 on each serving plate. Place the juices in a small pot and reduce the liquid by half on your stovetop over medium high heat. Whisk in the butter and season with salt, pepper, lemon juice, and parsley. Spoon the sauce over the calamari.

PREP **40 MINUTES**
COOK **15 MINUTES**
SERVES **6**

fig **155**

WHITE WATER CLAMS
with piquillo pepper broth and smoked bacon

1 bag	small clams *(50 count)*
6 oz	piquillo pepper purée *(see pg. 171)*
2	red peppers
1 lb	apple wood smoked bacon
1 bunch	parsley
4	garlic cloves
2 cups	white wine
3 cups	fish stock *(see pg. 169)*
½ lb	butter
2	lemons *(juiced)*

Wash the clams in cold water to remove any sand. Store the clams in the refrigerator covered with a damp cloth. Do not keep the clams submerged in water for long periods of time.

Slice the bacon into 1/8" slices and sauté them in a large pot over medium high heat. Remove the bacon when it is crispy and reserve to finish the dish. Discard most of the grease in the pan except for 2 tablespoons. Slice thin strips of the red pepper flesh and sauté them in the bacon grease. Slice the garlic into paper-thin slices and sauté them with the peppers until they are golden brown. Add the clams and then deglaze with the wine. Add the fish stock and pepper purée. Cover the clams and steam for 6 minutes. Remove the cover to reduce the liquid and add the parsley and butter. Season the broth with salt, pepper, and juice of both lemons.

Place the clams in serving bowls and spoon the broth on top. Garnish with the crispy bacon.

PREP **20 MINUTES**
COOK **10 MINUTES**
SERVES **6**

OCTOPUS SALAD

with cured olives, arugula, and lemon olive oil

1	octopus *(2 lb)*
1	yellow onion
2 ribs	celery
1 bulb	fennel
1 head	garlic
1 bunch	parsley
2	jalapeño peppers

3 ribs	celery
1	red onion *(small)*
2	cucumber
8 oz	cured Greek olives *(roughly chopped)*
2	tomatoes
1 bunch	arugula
6 leaves	basil

3	lemons
½ cup	extra virgin olive oil

Chop the onion, jalapeño, and celery and place them in a large stock pot with salted water. Trim the fennel and dice 1 cup of nice fennel for the salad. Place the other pieces of fennel in the water with the vegetables. Cut a head of garlic in half and add it to the water as well as the parsley. Bring the mixture to a boil and turn down to simmer for 10 minutes. Wash the octopus in cold water and massage it to slightly tenderize. Place it in the simmering stock pot and cook it for 40 minutes. It should be tender by this time. Transfer the octopus to a strainer to cool. Slice the octopus into bite-size pieces and keep refrigerated until needed.

In a bowl with the cup of reserved fennel, add the diced celery, red onion, and olives. Remove the skin and seeds from the tomatoes and dice them as well. Peel, de-seed and chop the flesh of the cucumber. Clean the arugula of the stems and mix it together with the salad. Zest the lemons and add it to the bowl with the juice. Fold in the olive oil, chopped basil, salt, and fresh cracked black pepper.

PREP 45 MINUTES
COOK 10 MINUTES
SERVES 6

Mix the octopus with the salad and serve chilled.

RAZOR CLAMS

with spicy tomato sauce

30	live razor clams
2	shallots *(minced)*
1 Tbs	chopped garlic
2 Tbs	olive oil
2 cup	pinot grigio
2 ½ cup	fish stock *(see pg. 169)*
4 oz	heavy cream
3 cups	spicy tomato sauce *(see pg. 171)*
1 Tbs	sherry vinegar

If you can get fresh razor clams in your neck of the woods, try them in this simple recipe. You could substitute any of your local clams. The big problem with razor clams is the gritty dirt they might have still in their shells if they have never been purged. If you look at them and they seem very sandy, you will have to clean them first. I blanch them in boiling water for 10 seconds and shock them in ice water to stop the cooking. You then pull out the meat and save the shells for presentation. The foot of the clam will have a hard cover that you can cut off and rinse the clam in cold water as you squeeze it to release any of the sand from the inside of the clam. You can cut them into smaller bite-size pieces as well. Feel free to cook them without any prior preparation. They will taste similar to a steamer clam.

Heat a large stainless steel sauté pan over medium high heat. Warm the olive oil in the pan and add the shallots and garlic. Sauté them until lightly brown and deglaze with the white wine. Put the clams in at this time and add the fish stock as well. Cover the dish for 2 minutes. Add the spicy tomato sauce. Cook for 1 more minute or until the clams are open. Swirl in the heavy cream and season with salt, pepper, and sherry vinegar. Place equal portions of the clams on six large platters.

PREP **25 MINUTES**
COOK **15 MINUTES**
SERVES **6**

GLOSSARY

SALT

I always tell my new cooks that using salt is like going to the Grand Canyon. You need to go to the edge to enjoy the best view, but when you go one step too far, you're finished. I never put down salt as an ingredient, however, I do let you know where to use it. Salt is like a cheerleader pushing the ingredient up to be noticed. So many people just make the simple mistake of not properly seasoning. It is not just my love for the salty ocean that makes this a staple in almost all of my dishes.

STOCKS

Stocks are the backbone for perfect sauce construction. They are a base to build on and their character defines each dish. We gently cook our stocks over time to extract a flavor and clarity that gives us the proper foundation. Cooking a stock too fast without skimming and straining leaves a cloudy and messy infusion.

AIOLI

Aioli is the basic mayonnaise we all know. The sauce stems from the blending of eggs and oil. To make numerous sauces, we simply adjust that base with different acidity and flavors. I like to keep these sauces a little looser than your typical mayonnaise. I like to make my sauce stronger in flavor and use less on the plate.

MODERN SAUCES

The most delicate part of the plate is the sauce. It should enhance the main components, but not cover up their flavor. In modern cuisine, we keep things light with vinaigrettes, vegetable juices, natural purées, and starchless reductions. We tend to use more broths, and froths rather than butter and cream. It is the thickeners of the past that add the heavy feel to a sauce and to your stomach. We reduce 20 gallons of chicken stock down to one gallon to make a flavorful juice with no starches.

JUICES

We use the juice or extractions of vegetables, fruits, and herbs to create modern sauces that showcase simplicity and boldness all in one. One of my favorite examples is the juice from cooked spinach. To serve the juice with a squeeze of lemon and drops of olive oil define simplicity. Reducing a juice can bring out sweetness and earthiness and can be used to balance a dish in a light and healthy way.

VINAIGRETTE

Vinaigrettes are great to add flavor, acidity, and lightness to a dish. It is almost the same as an aioli without the egg. Mostly vinaigrettes are not a smooth emulsion, but a separation of juice and oil. The juice is the intense flavor and the oil is there to balance. Most people see them just as salad dressings, but I see them as a complete sauce that can prevail in any dish.

BASIC RECIPES :: SAUCES

ORGANIC BEET CREAM

The simple sweetness of this sauce is only as good as the beets involved. The finished product will be a fantastic creamy pink addition to a dish that needs a touch of fattiness.

    2 large red beets
      (or 1 cup beet juice)
    2 shallots
½ cup white wine
1 cup fish stock (see pg. 169)
    1 bay leaf
    1 sprig of thyme
1 cup heavy cream
 1 tsp sherry vinegar

Wash the beets of any dirt. Cut them into small pieces. Juice the beets in a vegetable juicer. Mince the shallots. Heat a tablespoon of olive oil in a small saucepot. Sauté the shallots for 1 minute and deglaze with the white wine. Reduce the wine until almost dry. Add the beet juice, fish stock, bay leaf, and thyme and reduce the mixture by two-thirds the original volume. Add the heavy cream and bring to a boil. Remove the bay leaf and thyme stem and purée the sauce in a blender. Season with salt, fresh ground white pepper, and the sherry vinegar.

Keep in the refrigerator until needed.

GREEN PEA SAUCE

The simplicity of this sauce is the smoothness the cream adds with the sweet spring flavor of peas. It is a quick sauce that showcases the peas strength.

    1 shallot
½ tsp garlic (chopped)
2 Tbs diced prosciutto scraps
1 Tbs butter
1 cup pea sprout stems
1 cup spinach leaves
1 cup white wine
1 cup heavy cream

In the restaurant, we have the end cuts from the prosciutto and the stems from the pea sprouts which add the flavor to the sauce. You could easily substitute some bacon and snap peas to make the same sauce.

In a small saucepan, heat the butter over a medium high heat. Chop the shallots and add them to the butter along with the garlic and prosciutto. Sauté the mixture for 1 minute. Add the pea stems and let them wilt for 1 minute. Deglaze with the white wine and reduce the mixture until the wine is gone. Add the cream and bring to a boil. Stir in the spinach and let it cook for 1 more minute. Transfer immediately to a blender and carefully blend the mixture until the sauce is smooth. Season with salt and white pepper. Strain the sauce and keep in a warm place until needed.

FRESH FISH CREAM

Fish cream is a great base to enhance many different fish dishes. The fresh fish flavor it brings to the plate is irreplaceable.

1 tsp	black peppercorns
1	bay leaf
2	shallots *(minced)*
2 Tbs	butter
¼ cup	white wine
1 oz	Noilly Prat
1 oz	white port
1 cup	fish stock *(see pg. 169)*
1½ cups	cream
2 Tbs	crème fraiche
	(can also substitute sour cream)

Sauté in a small saucepot the peppercorns, bay leaf, and shallots with the butter. Add the wine, port, and Noilly Prat. Cook until the liquid is gone. Add the fish stock and reduce by half. Add the cream and bring it to a boil. Simmer the cream for a couple of minutes and add the crème fraiche. Purée the mixture. Strain the cream and season with salt.

YIELDS **2 CUPS**

GRAINY MUSTARD SAUCE

This cream based sauce gets a balance from the spiciness of the mustard and sweetness of the Riesling. This is another example of how we use the fresh fish cream as a base to many variations.

2 Tbs	high-quality grainy mustard
½ cup	Riesling wine
1 Tbs	honey
1 cup	fresh fish cream

In a small saucepot, bring to a boil the wine, honey, and mustard. Reduce the mixture by half, and add in the cream. Bring the cream to a boil, simmer for another 2-3 minutes. Season with salt and white pepper.

YIELDS **1 CUP**

CHICKEN STOCK

Chicken stock is a great base for the construction of many sauces, including seafood themes. Sometimes the use of fish stock can be too overwhelming, and a more comforting chicken stock works better.

5 lbs	chicken bones
½ cup	onion *(chopped)*
½ cup	celery *(chopped)*
½ cup	carrot *(chopped)*
½ cup	tomato *(chopped)*
½ cup	leek *(chopped)*
1 bunch	parsley
1 bunch	thyme
1 head	garlic *(halved)*
2 Tbs	salt
2 Tbs	whole black pepper
2	bay leaves
1½ gal	cold water

Roast the chicken bones in a 350° oven for 10 minutes. Add the vegetables to the chicken and roast for 10 minutes more. Place all the ingredients in a large stock pot with the water. Bring the stock to a boil and skim the surface to remove any fat or scum. Turn the stock down to a very gentle simmer and continue to cook for 6-8 hours. If you skim the stock well in the beginning, you can leave it alone till the end of the cooking time. When the stock is done, strain it into a large container and let it set at room temperature for 10 minutes to cool. Skim any fat that has settled on the top. You could add a bottle of white wine to this recipe if you have some old dry wine around the house. Place the cooled stock in the refrigerator until needed. You can freeze the stock in 2 cup batches for ease of use.

COURT BOUILLON

This stock is simply a flavorful broth in which to cook lobsters, shrimp, and other seafood items. We tend to make the flavor much too intense to drink as a soup since it will need to leave its impact on the item cooking.

2 cups	onion *(chopped)*
1 cup	leek *(chopped)*
1 cup	carrot *(chopped)*
1 cup	celery *(chopped)*
1 cup	fennel *(chopped)*
1 bulb	garlic *(halved)*
6 sprigs	fresh thyme, tarragon, and parsley
2 Tbs	black peppercorns
2	stars anise *(can also substitute fennel seed)*
4 Tbs	sea salt
2	lemons *(zest and juice)*
1 cup	dry white wine
1½ gal	water

Bring the above ingredients to a boil in a large stockpot. Reduce the bouillon by one-third and strain into a large container. Reserve until needed.

VEAL STOCK

The meaty flavor of veal stock makes a great match with some fish. I make a light and clear veal stock using less tomato. Veal stock can be a great vehicle for flavor with very little fat. It allows the dish to remain light and delicate.

5 lbs	veal bones
½ cup ea	onion, carrot, celery, leek *(chopped)*
1 bunch	thyme
1 bunch	parsley
1 bulb	garlic *(halved)*
½ cup	tomato *(chopped)*
2 Tbs	tomato paste
2 Tbs	salt
2	bay leaves
2 Tbs	black peppercorn
2 gal	water
½ bottle	leftover dry red wine

Roast the veal bones in a heavy pan in the oven at 400 degrees until they are a golden color. Add the onions, carrots, celery, leeks and tomato paste to the bones and roast for 15 more minutes. Remove the pan from the oven and place the bones and vegetables in a large stockpot. Pour off the grease from the pan and deglaze it with the red wine. Scrape the pan clean with a flat spatula and place the wine and scrapings in the stockpot with the bones and vegetables. Add the cold water and remaining ingredients. Bring the stock to a boil and turn it down to a slow simmer. Cook the stock at this speed for at least 20 hours. After the first hour, skim the fat off the top of the stock. When the stock has cooked down by half, strain the liquid and discard the solids. Let the stock cool while periodically skimming it. To keep this stock for future use, reduce the gallon of veal stock down to half its volume. Then store it in 1 cup batches in the freezer.

YIELDS 1 GALLON

FISH STOCK

A light fish stock can be a great base to enhance a variety of sauces. The key to a fish stock is to gently infuse the flavor of the bones in the liquid, giving you a light, and clear broth. It is better to use mild fish bones from white fleshed lean fish like snapper, halibut, grouper, and flounder. Stock from oily fish like salmon would be too overpowering.

5 lbs	white fish bones
1 cup	onion *(chopped)*
½ cup	celery *(chopped)*
½ cup	leek *(chopped)*
½ bulb	fennel *(chopped)*
2 Tbs	olive oil
4 sprigs	dill, thyme, and parsley
2	bay leaves
1 bulb	garlic *(halved)*
1 Tbs	white peppercorns
2 Tbs	sea salt
½ bottle	white wine
1 cup	vermouth
1 gal	water

Wash the bones in cold water to remove any blood that is on them. Gently sauté the onions, celery, leeks, fennel, garlic, salt, bay leaf, peppercorns, and herbs with the olive oil. When the vegetables have wilted you can deglaze with the wine and vermouth, until the liquid is almost dry. Add the cold water and bring the stock to a boil. Turn down to a very gentle simmer, and skim the scum that floats to the surface. Cook the stock for no more than 45 minutes. Turn the stock off and let it infuse off the heat for 30 minutes. Ladle the clear stock through a strainer and discard any of the cloudy solids at the bottom of the pot. This stock can be frozen in small batches until needed.

YIELDS 1 GALLON

ROASTED SWEET PEPPER SAUCE

This creamy sauce gets its body from the bright, sweet flavor of the roasted peppers. It adds a sweet, spicy, and creamy flavor to any dish.

4	sweet red bell or lipstick peppers
1	shallot
3 Tbs	olive oil
1 Tbs	garlic *(chopped)*
1 Tbs	paprika
2 Tbs	honey
2 Tbs	Champagne vinegar
1½ cups	chicken stock
1 cup	cream

Peel and roughly cut the peppers into chunky pieces. Mince the shallot. Roast the peppers with the olive oil in a 350 degree oven for 10 minutes using an ovenproof sauté pan. Add the shallots, garlic and paprika and mix it with the peppers. Continue roasting for an additional 10 minutes. Take the sauté pan out of the oven and on to a medium high burner. Add the honey and let it cook for a minute. Deglaze with the vinegar and then add the chicken stock. Reduce by half. Add the cream and bring it to a boil. Purée the sauce in a blender and season with salt and white pepper. Press the sauce through a fine strainer.

PICKLING JUICE

Pickling juice can be used to give a sweet marinated flavor and more gentle texture to many different vegetables. It is great with radishes, cucumbers, carrots, and many more.

2	shallots *(minced)*
½ cup	onion *(chopped)*
½ cup	carrot *(chopped)*
1	garlic bulb *(halved)*
3	jalapeño peppers *(chopped)*
1 Tbs ea	mustard seeds, black pepper and coriander seeds
2	bay leaves
1 tsp	cloves
1 cup	sugar
2 cups	Champagne vinegar
2 cups	water

You can feel free to adjust the flavorings of the juice by adding more regional spices and making the marinade more or less spicy by the amount and type of pepper you include.

Boil all the ingredients for 5 minutes. Let the mixture cool at room temperature giving it time to steep. When the liquid has cooled, you can pass it through a fine strainer. Keep it refrigerated until needed.

ROASTED PIQUILLO PURÉE

This small Mediterranean sweet pepper has a gentle spiciness which makes it very popular in its region. You could substitute red bell peppers or lipstick peppers.

12	piquillo peppers *or*
6	red bell peppers
1 Tbs	garlic confit
6 Tbs	extra virgin olive oil
1	lemon

Rub the peppers with 1 tablespoon of olive oil. Season them with salt and pepper. Roast them whole in a 350 degree oven for 15 minutes. Remove the peppers and wrap them in plastic while they cool. When they are cool enough to handle, peel the skin and discard it with the stem and seeds. Place the cleaned flesh in a blender with the garlic and juice of the lemon. Purée the peppers while drizzling in the 5 tablespoons of olive oil. Season with salt. Store in the refrigerator until needed.

SPICY TOMATO SAUCE

This spicy tomato sauce is a great base to have in the freezer for quick sauces for pasta and seafood. If you are not a big spicy fan, you can do this without the chili paste.

3 cups	vine ripe tomatoes *(peeled, seeded, and chopped)*
2	shallots *(minced)*
1	yellow onion *(chopped)*
1 Tbs	garlic *(minced)*
pinch	saffron
1 Tbs	sambal chili paste
6 Tbs	olive oil
2 cups	chicken stock

SACHET OF:

1 Tbs	fennel seeds
1	bay leaf
6 sprigs	thyme
6 sprigs	basil

Heat a sauce skillet over a medium high heat. Add the oil and let it warm. Sauté the onions and shallots in the oil for 2 minutes. Add in the garlic and chili paste and let it cook for another minute. Put the pinch of saffron, tomatoes, and chicken stock in the mixture. Wrap up a sachet of cheese cloth with the fennel, bay leaf, thyme, and basil. Place it in the tomato sauce. Bring the mixture to a boil and turn it down to a medium simmer. Reduce the sauce until the stock has reduced by two-thirds. Season with fresh pepper and salt. Let the sauce cool and freeze until needed.

LOBSTER STOCK

Lobster stock should be made with the left over heads from any lobster dinners you have had in the past. If you do not have the time to make it that day, you can simply freeze the heads until you are ready to proceed. The key to this stock is to simmer the stock for no longer than an hour to keep it from turning bitter. Let the shells steep in the liquid before straining.

6	Maine lobster heads and shells
6 Tbs	olive oil
1 cup ea	onion, celery, carrot, fennel *(chopped)*
½ cup	leek *(chopped)*
1 ea	garlic bulb *(halved)*, bay leaf
1 bunch	thyme
4	stars anise
1 Tbs	fennel seeds
1 cup	tomato *(chopped)*
4 Tbs	tomato paste
½ bottle	dry white wine
4 oz	Cognac
1 gal	chicken stock
4 cups	water

Heat a large stock pot over a medium high flame. Crush and chop the lobster shells and heads into small pieces with a butcher's cleaver. Keep any juice that comes from the lobster. Put the olive oil in the hot stock pot. Stir in the lobster shells and sauté them for 4 minutes. Add the onion, celery, carrot, fennel, leek, and garlic and cook for 4 more minutes. Deglaze with the cognac and then add the white wine, bay leaf, thyme, star anise, fennel seeds, tomatoes, and tomato paste. Reduce the wine until it is dry. Cover the shells with the water and chicken stock, and bring to a boil. Turn down the stock and simmer for 45 minutes. Turn the stock off and let it cool at room temperature. When the stock has completely cooled, strain the juice through a fine strainer while pressing the solids for every bit of its nectar. Store the stock in small batches in the freezer until needed.

YIELDS 1 GALLON

GARLIC CONFIT

Garlic is such a great aromatic root and those who love it live by it. Even though I do like the use of raw garlic sparingly, it can leave you with an upset stomach and really bad breath. The sweet flavor of cooked garlic that you get from this confit can be used anywhere from vinaigrettes to a spread for bread. You can make a large batch and use bits of it out of your refrigerator for weeks.

2 cups	cleaned garlic cloves
1 cup	extra virgin olive oil
1 Tbs	sea salt
1 Tbs	cracked white pepper

Place the garlic cloves in a small pot with the olive oil, salt, and pepper. Cook the garlic for 30 minutes over the lowest flame on your stove top. Test the garlic by pressing it with a fork. It should mash with no resistance. Transfer the garlic to a blender and purée it while drizzling in the olive oil that was cooked with it. Press the garlic paste through a strainer to yield a smooth purée of golden sweet garlic. Put this paste in a air tight jar and refrigerate until needed.

YIELDS 1 CUP

GARLIC AIOLI

This is a simple sauce that is great for a million uses.

1 whole egg
1 lemon
3 Tbs Champagne vinegar
3 Tbs garlic confit
1 tsp Dijon mustard
¾ cup grape seed oil
¼ cup extra virgin olive oil

Put the egg, lemon juice, vinegar, garlic, and mustard in a blender and purée for 30 seconds. Drizzle in the oil slowly while the blender is on a medium speed. As the sauce begins to thicken, carefully help it to move in the blender with a rubber spatula. Be very careful not to let the blades of the blender hit the spatula. Season the sauce with salt and cracked pepper. Store in the refrigerator until needed.

WHITE TRUFFLE AIOLI

White truffle works like garlic aioli giving the sauce a distinguishable earthiness.

1 whole egg
3 Tbs Champagne vinegar
2 Tbs white truffle oil
1 tsp Dijon mustard
¾ cup grape seed oil
¼ cup extra virgin olive oil

Put the egg, vinegar, truffle oil, and mustard in a blender and purée for 30 seconds. Drizzle in the oil slowly while the blender is on a medium speed. As the sauce begins to thicken, carefully help it to move in the blender with a rubber spatula. Be very careful not to let the blades of the blender hit the spatula. Season the sauce with salt. Store in the refrigerator until needed.

BASIL AIOLI

The summer flavor that basil envokes makes this aioli a great sauce to accompany grilled items.

1 whole egg
1 lemon
3 Tbs Champagne vinegar
1 cup basil leaves
1 Tbs Dijon mustard
¾ cup grape seed oil
¼ cup basil olive oil

Blanch the basil leaves in boiling water for 10 seconds and place them quickly into ice water. Dry the basil and place it in the blender with the egg, lemon juice, vinegar, and mustard and purée for 30 seconds. Drizzle in the oil slowly while the blender is on a medium speed. As the sauce begins to thicken, carefully help it to move in the blender with a rubber spatula. Be very careful not to let the blades of the blender hit the spatula. Season the sauce with salt. Store in the refrigerator until needed.

YIELDS 1 CUP

CUMIN MINT AIOLI

The mixture of mint and cumin give this aioli an interesting flair. It is lightly spicy and subtly exotic.

1 whole egg
1 lemon
3 Tbs Champagne vinegar
2 Tbs toasted and ground cumin seeds
1 cup mint leaves
1 tsp Dijon mustard
1 cup grape seed oil

Blanch the mint leaves in boiling water for 10 seconds and place them quickly into ice water. Dry the mint and place it in the blender with the egg, lemon juice, vinegar, cumin and mustard and purée for 30 seconds. Drizzle in the oil slowly while the blender is on a medium speed. As the sauce begins to thicken, carefully help it to move in the blender with a rubber spatula. Be very careful not to let the blades of the blender hit the spatula. Season the sauce with salt. Store in the refrigerator until needed.

YIELDS 1 CUP

COCONUT CURRY SAUCE

This tropical flavored sauce is a perfect balance of spicy ginger and curry with the sweetness of the sugar cutting the heat of the chili. The creamy enchanting presence of the coconut really makes this soar with any delicate seafood item.

2 Tbs	peanut oil
2 ea	green onions, shallots
1	fresh ginger *(1-inch piece)*
4 cloves	garlic *(smashed)*
1 stalk	lemon grass *(smashed and chopped)*
1	Thai chili *(chopped)*, bayleaf
1 tbs	red Thai curry paste
6 Tbs	brown sugar
1 cup	vermouth
2 cups	chicken stock
2 can	coconut milk
1 tsp	whole coriander seeds
2 sprigs	thyme
1	lime *(juiced)*
½ cup	cilantro leaves *(chopped)*

In a small saucepot, gently saute the green onion, shallot, ginger, garlic, lemongrass with the peanut oil for a couple of minutes. Add in the curry paste and chili and continue to cook for a few minutes more. Next, put in the herbs and spices and brown sugar and cook for two more minutes. Deglaze with vermouth, and when it has cooked completely dry, add in the chicken stock and simmer for ten minutes, or until reduced by half. Pour in the coconut milk and bring it to a boil. Remove the sauce from the heat and let it cool at room temperature. Purée the sauce in a blender and strain it through a fine sieve. Reheat the sauce when needed and finish it with fresh cilantro, lime juice, and salt.

SPICY MUSTARD AIOLI

The balance of spicy and sweet in this aioli make it a perfect match with chilled lobster, crab, and shrimp.

1	egg
1	lemon
1 Tbs	Champagne vinegar
1 Tbs	honey
1 tsp	Dijon mustard
3 dash	Tabasco sauce
1 tsp	cayenne pepper
¾ cup	grape seed oil
¼ cup	mustard oil *(from specialty grocer)*

Put the egg, lemon juice, vinegar, honey, cayenne, Tabasco, and mustard in a blender and purée for 30 seconds. Drizzle in the oil slowly while the blender is on a medium speed. As the sauce begins to thicken, carefully help it to move in the blender with a rubber spatula. Be very careful not to let the blades of the blender hit the spatula. Season the sauce with salt and cracked pepper. Store in the refrigerator until needed.

CURRY APPLE AIOLI

The balance of a sweet apple with spicy curry make this an interesting aioli for many combinations.

1	green apple
1 Tbs	Madras curry powder
1	shallot *(minced)*
1 oz	Calvados liquor *(optional)*
1	egg
2 Tbs	apple cider vinegar
1 tsp	Dijon mustard
¾ cups	grape seed oil
¼ cup	turmeric oil
	(grape seed oil with 1 Tbs turmeric)

Peel, and slice the apple. Sauté the apple and shallots with a tablespoon of the grape seed oil in a small pan over medium heat. After 2 minutes, stir in the curry powder and cook for 1 more minute. Deglaze with the Calvados. Let the mixture cool. Put the egg, apple shallot mixture, vinegar, and mustard in a blender and purée for 30 seconds. Drizzle in the oil slowly while the blender is on a medium speed. As the sauce begins to thicken, carefully help it to move in the blender with a rubber spatula. Be very careful not to let the blades of the blender hit the spatula. Season the sauce with salt. Store in the refrigerator until needed.

YIELDS 1 CUP

SPICY CHILI AIOLI

The Asian flavors in this aioli make it a great match for tempura vegetables and fish. Its also a great pair with mild flavor seviche.

1	egg
1	lime
1 Tbs	rice wine vinegar
1 Tbs	sesame paste
2 Tbs	soy sauce
1 Tbs	fresh ginger *(minced)*
2 Tbs	mirin
2 Tbs	sambal chili paste
1 tsp	wasabi paste
1 cups	grape seed oil
¼ cup	sesame oil

Put the egg, lime juice, vinegar, sesame paste, soy sauce, ginger, mirin, chili paste, and wasabi in a blender and purée for 30 seconds. Drizzle in the oil slowly while the blender is on a medium speed. As the sauce begins to thicken, carefully help it to move in the blender with a rubber spatula. Be very careful not to let the blades of the blender hit the spatula. Season the sauce with salt. Store in the refrigerator until needed.

YIELDS 2 CUPS

LEMON VINAIGRETTE

This basic vinaigrette is a great blend to add an acidic jolt to simple greens or grilled vegetables.

½ cup fresh lemon juice
½ Tbs sea salt
1 tsp ground white pepper
2 Tbs black truffle oil
2 Tbs Champagne vinegar
¾ cup extra virgin olive oil

Whisk in a bowl all the ingredients and keep in the refrigerator until needed.

BLACK OLIVE VINAIGRETTE

This is a pungent vinaigrette that is very Mediterranean, and hard to pair outside that realm. It's a great balance of acidity with very distinct flavors.

3 Tbs lemon juice
1 Tbs sea salt
1 tsp ground white pepper
¼ cup pitted black olives
2 anchovy fillets
1 Tbs capers
1 Tbs garlic confit
3 Tbs Champagne vinegar
¾ cups extra virgin olive oil

Purée in the blender all the ingredients except the oil. When a nice paste has formed, drizzle in the olive oil. Keep in the refrigerator until needed.

GREEN OLIVE VINAIGRETTE

This chunky vinaigrette would actually border a salsa. The sweet acidic peppery flavor pairs well with both fish and meats.

½ cup picholine olives *(pitted and chopped)*
1 red onion *(finely diced)*
1 red pepper *(finely diced)*
2 tomatoes *(peeled, and finely diced)*
1 yellow pepper *(finely diced)*
1 jalapeño pepper *(finely diced)*
1 Tbs garlic confit
2 Tbs lemon juice
2 Tbs Champagne vinegar
1 Tbs sea salt
2 Tbs ground pepper
1 bunch cilantro *(leaves picked and chopped)*
¼ cup extra virgin olive oil

Combine all the ingredients and refrigerate until needed.

VODKA BEET VINAIGRETTE

This vinaigrette has a very northern European feel and would be good with many cold weather seafood items.

1 cup fresh beet juice
1 shallot *(minced)*
1 Tbs juniper berries
1 bay leaf
1 oz vodka
1 Tbs lemon juice
2 Tbs balsamic vinegar
¾ cup extra virgin olive oil

Reduce the beet juice, shallots, juniper, and bay leaf until there is only 1/4 cup of liquid left. Strain the mixture and whisk in the vodka, lemon juice, balsamic, and olive oil. Season with salt and fresh ground black pepper.

SOY VINAIGRETTE

The distinctive balance of these Japanese flavors make this great with sashimi and crispy seafood.

2 Tbs	fresh grated wasabi root
¼ cup	soy sauce
1 Tbs	brown sugar
2	green onions *(chopped)*
1	serrano chili *(chopped)*
2 Tbs	mirin
4 Tbs	rice wine vinegar
¼ cup	sesame oil
¾ cup	grape seed oil

Warm the wasabi, soy, sugar, onions, and chili gently together and reduce down to 4 tablespoons of liquid. Strain the mixture and whisk in the mirin, vinegar, sesame oil, and grape seed oil.

YIELDS 1 CUP

PASSION FRUIT SAUCE

The pungent flavor of passion fruit acts as a strong character in which to balance other powerful flavors.

½ cup	passion fruit purée
1	Scotch bonnet pepper *(chopped with no seeds)*
1 Tbs	minced shallot
4 Tbs	sugar
3 Tbs	lime juice
½ cup	extra virgin olive oil

Gently warm the passion fruit, pepper, shallot, and sugar and cook the mixture for 5 minutes. Strain the juice and whisk in the lime and oil. Season with sea salt.

YIELDS 1 CUP

RED WINE VINAIGRETTE

The acidic, sweet, and floral flavor of the red wine make this an interesting addition to many earthy combinations.

2 cups red wine
1 bay leaf
1 Tbs minced shallot
1 sprig thyme
1 Tbs sugar
1 Tbs red wine vinegar
½ cup extra virgin olive oil

Reduce the red wine, bayleaf, shallot, thyme, and sugar until a 1/4 cup of liquid is left. Strain the mixture and whisk in the red wine vinegar and olive oil. Season with salt and pepper.

FLORIDA CITRUS SAUCE

The mixture of all these distinctive acidic fruits give a great tropical flare to any dish. Its light feel makes it a great pair with fried and grilled seafood.

1 grapefruit
2 oranges
1 lemon
1 lime
1 tangerine
2 kumquats
1 stalk lemongrass *(chopped)*
1 Tbs fresh chopped ginger
1 Tbs coriander seeds
1 Tbs fennel seeds
2 shallots *(minced)*
2 Tbs rice vinegar
2 Tbs fresh pressed peanut oil
¾ cup grape seed oil

Zest, segment, and juice the grapefruit, oranges, lemon, lime, and tangerine. Thinly slice the kumquats and remove their seeds. Place the segments and the kumquats in a bowl. Place the citrus juice, zest, ginger, lemongrass, coriander, fennel, and shallots in a small pot to reduce over a medium flame. When the juice has reduced to just before a paste, press it through a fine mesh strainer. Add it to the bowl with the segments and whisk in the vinegar and oils. Season with salt and fresh ground pepper.

SOY CITRUS JUICE

This clean, refreshing juice is a perfect flavor balance for sashimi, pickled vegetables, and tempura.

½ cup fresh squeezed orange juice
        (strained)
 2 Tbs mirin
 2 Tbs lemon Juice
¼ cup soy sauce

Squeeze the oranges in a bowl and leave one of the halves of orange in the juice to marinate. Add the mirin, lemon juice and soy sauce. Refrigerate the mixture for 2 hours and strain the juice into a bottle. Keep refrigerated until needed.

YIELDS 1 CUP

SWEET SOY GLAZE

This teriyaki style glaze is perfect for adding a salty sweetness to grilled fish. It also helps to maintain moisture when grilling leaner fish.

½ cup apricot preserves
½ cup soy sauce
 1 Tbs sesame oil
 2 Tbs ginger *(minced)*
 2 Tbs ketjap manis
        (Indonesian soy, optional)

Warm the apricot, soy, sesame, ginger, and manis in a small pot over a low heat for 10 minutes. Whisk the mixture occasionally to create a smooth glaze. Press the glaze through a fine strainer and keep refrigerated until needed.

YIELDS 1 CUP

BLACK BEAN SAUCE

The distinctive flavor of fermented black beans give this sauce an interesting dimension. Its feel is truly for Asian style items.

½ cup fermented black beans
2 shallots *(minced)*
2 Tbs fresh ginger *(chopped)*
2 Tbs garlic *(minced)*
1 cup chicken stock
2 Tbs ketjap manis
(Indonesian soy, optional)
2 Tbs butter

Rinse the beans in cold water. Sauté the shallots, ginger, and garlic with the butter over a medium high heat. Add in the black beans and deglaze with the chicken stock and soy sauce. Simmer the mixture for 5 minutes. Keep the sauce warm until needed.

PARSLEY PURÉE AND OIL

Flat leaf, or better known as Italian parsley, has a beautiful and delicate flavor that can really make a dish shine. The parsley purée or its oil can be a great way to give a dish a more summery or Mediterranean feel.

2 bunches parsley *(pick leaves only)*
1 cup extra virgin olive oil

Blanch the parsley by plunging it in boiling water for 20 seconds and then shocking it in ice water. Squeeze the water from the parsley and purée it in a blender with the olive oil until smooth. Season the purée with salt and white pepper.

For parsley oil, warm one cup of parsley purée until it begins to bubble and is close to a boil. Remove the purée from the heat and strain it through a fine sieve. Let the mixture cool in a glass container until it has separated. Skim the green parsley oil from the top and discard the juice on the bottom.

SUN CHOKE RAVIOLI

*Making ravioli is simple and fun. There is no substitute for a fresh
handmade dough. This dough is delicate yet hardy. Try it with
any filling.*

DOUGH:

2 cups	"00" imported pasta flour
4	egg yolks
3	whole eggs
1 Tbs	extra virgin olive oil
2 tsp	salt

FILLING:

1 lb	sun chokes
1 cup	milk
1	lemon
2 Tbs	salt
1 Tbs	butter
1 Tbs	white truffle oil

EGG WASH:

2	whole eggs
1 Tbs	milk
	(mixed together)

PREP **50 MINUTES**
COOK **15 MINUTES**
SERVES **6**

First make the ravioli dough since it will need time to rest. In a large bowl make a small well in the mound of pasta flour. Put the eggs, oil and salt in the well. Mix the eggs with a fork until blended and start folding in the flour. When the pasta has formed a ball, work it with the ball of your hand until the mixture is smoothly mixed. Wrap the dough in plastic and place it in the refrigerator.

Put the peeled sun chokes in a medium stainless steel pot with the milk, lemon juice, salt, and enough cold water to cover. Bring the sun chokes to a boil and simmer for 15 minutes until cooked through. Drain the sun chokes and place them in a food processor with the butter and truffle oil. Blend them into a smooth paste. Season with salt and ground white pepper. Cool the sun choke purée in the refrigerator.

Cut dough into 6 workable pieces. With pasta machine, roll the dough out starting on the widest setting and getting the pasta as thin as possible without creating holes. Always flour the dough between each rolling process to keep it from sticking on the machine. Lay the pasta sheets on a flat work surface and place a tablespoon of the chilled sun choke purée on top. Make the piles of purée at least 3 inches apart to give space to make the ravioli. Brush the pasta with the egg wash and place another sheet of pasta on top. Press down around the sun choke purée to get out any air pockets. Cut the ravioli with your favorite cutter. Flour the ravioli and keep them in the refrigerator uncovered. If you make them more than 10 hours before needed you can keep them in an airtight container in the freezer.

FRESH SUMMER WATERMELON MARTINI

The beauty of this martini lies in the perfection of fresh watermelon juice. There is no substitute!

15 oz. premium vodka
18 oz. fresh pressed watermelon juice
      (juiced not puréed)
 6 oz. sugar
 3 oz. water
    1 lime *(juiced)*
1 cup ice

 1 oz. sugar
 1 oz. Salt

Dissolve the sugar with hot water and let that cool in the refrigerator. Mix the vodka, watermelon, sugar mixture, lime juice, and ice in a large shaker. Shake the mixture very well. Chill the martini glasses in the freezer. Rub the rims of the glasses with the already squeezed lime and dip the rim of the glass into the sugar and salt mixture.

Strain the martini into the rimmed glasses and serve very cold.

PREP 10 MINUTES
COOK 3 MINUTES
SERVES 6

FLORIDA KEY LIME MARTINI

A trip to South Florida would not be the same without the experience of our treasured key lime. Everybody has had the pie, but why not put the pie in a glass?

15 oz. premium vodka
 6 oz. key lime liquor
 6 oz. melon liquor
    6 key limes *(juiced)*
 9 oz. cream

    graham crackers *(crushed)*

Mix the vodka in a large shaker with key lime liquor, melon liquor, key lime juice, and cream. Shake the mixture very well. Chill the martini glasses in the freezer. Rub the rims of the glasses with the already squeezed lime and dip the rim of the glass into the crushed graham cracker crumbs.

Strain the martini into the rimmed glasses and serve very cold.

PREP 2 MINUTES
COOK 2 MINUTES
SERVES 6

To all my staff over the years who have supported and executed a vision of culinary excellence. A special thanks to my sous chef, Paula DaSilva, whose drive for perfection makes it possible for me to leave the building. I thank my cooks, Peter Forte, Glen Carnegie, Huma Nagi, Niven Patel, Julie Morales, Maria Herrera, Michael Clark, and Eric Wollmar for all their hard work and recipe tasting.

I also thank John Hearns who pushed me to do this book and gave me the creative freedom to make it happen.

I thank all my purveyors whose products I can't live without and whose relationships I treasure.

A thanks to my Restaurant Manager, Nicole Jackson, and all the front of house staff who put up with my obsessive personality. Their focus, patience, and tolerance makes every guest's experience a special one.

INDEX

Opposite page, clockwise from top left:
creamy mussel and clam with pasta.
Chef Dean examining the final product.
Working with my line cook, Garrett. Storing
fish for service. 3030 manager Nicole Jackson,
with my sous chef, Paula DaSilva, putting on
the final touches.

INDEX